Bugkiller

A Cropdusters Life

Ron Rounds ATP/ CFI/A&P IA

Order this book online at www.trafford.com
or email orders@trafford.com

Most Trafford titles are also available at major online book retailers.

For Glenn Souza, he served his country, his city, and his family
Above and beyond the call of duty.
Thanks for your friendship, Encouragement, and the cover graphic.....

Print information available on the last page.

ISBN: 978-1-4251-9006-4 (sc)

Because of the dynamic nature of the Internet, any web addresses or links contained in
this book may have changed since publication and may no longer be valid. The views
expressed in this work are solely those of the author and do not necessarily reflect the
views of the publisher, and the publisher hereby disclaims any responsibility for them.

Any people depicted in stock imagery provided by Getty Images are models, and such
images are being used for illustrative purposes only.
Certain stock imagery © Getty Images.

Trafford rev. 10/09/2018

www.trafford.com
North America & international
toll-free: 1 888 232 4444 (USA & Canada)
fax: 812 355 4082

Dedication

Crop dusting is a dangerous business. This book is dedicated to those killed while flying as an aerial applicator journeyman, more commonly known as a crop duster. They killed bugs, not people, in an attempt to provide food for your table, fiber for our clothing, and a host of other products for millions. They served in air combat of a different kind no less dedicated than the famous air aces, yet their names are unknown. A colorful band of brothers, fiercely competitive, and hard working, I am proud to have been counted in their ranks.

Acknowledgements

My thanks to all the ag pilots I have known and flown with over the years. With few exceptions, all were night crop dusters in the southwest. Some are still living and flying and some are as aviators say, gone west to the big hangar to learn from the master aviator. Thanks to the mechanics working on smelly, corroded, broken, contrary, aircraft and engines. There was never enough time and the conditions were always difficult, to every man you did a great job. Thanks to the families of the crews, loaders and flaggers that spent long nights at home alone while we sprayed everything in sight. Many thanks to the chasers that found and lighted the fields on pitch black nights; you bolstered my confidence and made my work easier... And last but not least my thanks to my wife Jeannie. Along with managing the home and kids, she flagged, washed airplanes, chased, did paperwork, and was my support system for all my years since high school.

Authors Note

I have tried to recount my experiences as accurately as possible. Some names have been changed to avoid embarrassment or indictment. This book started out as a chronology for my great grandchildren, Chris, Nick, and Mariah. I hope this will add to their sense of family history. It ended up being a little more than that.

Table of Contents

Introduction
A New Life

Not everyone knows where he or she came from. I never knew my biological father. I have some information but my efforts to find out more have not yielded much useful information. I have picked up bits and pieces from relatives over the years and I can only fabricate what I think happened from tiny pieces of information. I have daydreamed about the tearful reunions of relatives long lost, and watched moist-eyed as mother/daughter and father/son reunite after many years past on TV shows and movies. However, it did not work that way for me. Over the years, I have talked with some relatives, acquaintances, and other bystanders and curious I asked about any information that would illuminate my dark past. At some point I decided that it was not very important except for the day when my great grand children will ask, "what were they like". Well, I can tell them about my life but not much beyond that. What follows is some truth and some speculation added to tie the whole mess together. She was beautiful! Someone you would notice in a crowd. She lived in poverty and when a band came to a local bar in town she could hardly wait to go dancing and drinking with her friends and forget her everyday life. She was one of several children that ate too much and took up space at a time when food and jobs were scarce. When she went dancing that evening, the band leader noticed her in the audience and at a break he offered her dinner and drink. As the evening wore on it became a pleasant experience for a change. She went home with the band leader that night and my older half-brother arrived nine months later. It was very tough for her, an unwed teen mother in those times, and a source of shame and liability for someone just looking for comfort and affection. Of course, the band left town with its leader and she was left alone. Then time passed and she met a local fellow at a dance that made her feel comfortable. He was older and a local hero and pilot that had flown combat in Europe in World War 1.

Photography was his business and her beauty had not passed unnoticed. He began to take pictures and one thing led to another. I was the result nine months later He did not stay long enough to see me enter the world. Of course, she could not afford one child much less two. Her brother and his wife were childless so within a few months of my arrival I was given up for adoption to the people I would call my Mom and Dad. My new mom and dad loved me as their own and we became a happy family unit. They gave me their values, which included work ethic, church, family gatherings (although none were actually related to me), and freedom from any kind of abuse.   It was a happy upbringing and my dad helped me to learn many vocational arts.   I learned to operate a ten-inch table saw at the age of nine.   I could pull ten-penny nails from boards my dad brought home; he paid me a penny a nail. He also helped me to build my first model airplane. He built one too, but his hands were large and he was constantly upset about his clumsiness in handling the small parts required to assemble the model. I loved to go to his work place where they built road rollers, cement mixers, and spray rigs. During the war, they built troop gliders. He helped the design process for barrage rockets of the type seen in WW2 movie newsreels.   On weekends, he built patios and wired electricity for friends and family. He had doctor friends that would sketch a tool or surgical instrument and he would make a stainless steel instrument to the drawing from scratch. He repaired his own cars and could build nearly anything he could make a drawing of.   He was always helping people with labor or money. For a Christmas present, he gave me a portable typewriter and he told me his dream for me was to go to college some day. I still have the Underwood portable typewriter.   He had been receiving treatments (systoscopic) for his urinary tract and was in pain a great deal of the time. He came home from work early one day screaming in pain. The doctor was called and he summoned an ambulance. We followed the ambulance to the hospital in a friend's car. When we got to the hospital my dad was dead on arrival. I became the man of the house at age 13. My mom went to school to be a nurse and worked full time while I lived mostly alone in my world of school, model planes, and my workshop in the garage. I maintained the house, ran a paper route, and fixed my mom's car. As soon as I could get a license, I bought an old Salsbury motor scooter which wasn't running and fixed it up. The world was my oyster and 50 cents worth of gas would take me any where I needed to go. I worked part time at the hobby shop, pumped gas at the local station, and delivered the Daily News. I always had a job of some kind and always had money in my pocket. I did not see my birth mother again for several years and when I did see her I was introduced to her as my aunt. She was married and had two sons; my half brothers, and she had kept my older brother. At that time, we played and had a great time but none of us knew we were brothers. One day my older brother rode me on the handlebars of his bike into a   small midwest town and took me to the hobby shop. The smells there were marvelous! A mixture of tobacco, fuel, banana oil, and balsa wood,. I was instantly under the spell of the miniature-flying world. New doors had been opened. Afterwards we rode out to a local flying site where all sorts of model airplanes were flying furiously like a hive of mad bees. I was absolutely thrilled with what I saw there. To this day, I think it was probably my older brother's influence that started me on my path to aviation. There was no communication from our family to theirs except on each of my birthdays I would receive a card for my birthday and Christmas. This went on for years and when my kids were grammar school age; my birth mother and her sister showed up one day and visited us. We lived in an inaccessible place in the desert so it was really a surprise when they showed up at our door.   I arranged to borrow an airplane and took them both up for a ride up and down the Colorado River. I did not see them again for many years. On a business trip, I was in the Midwest and took a side trip to the town where my birth mother lived and I went to visit where she resided in a home. I took pictures of my family, which now included great grand sons. She was very elderly and didn't seem interested so I offered to take her out to lunch and she declined. So I said my good-byes and made my exit. I have not heard from her since that day. Perhaps I was conceived out of violence or some other unhappy circumstance. Whatever the case it was apparently something to be forgotten and I let the matter drop. I later heard that she passed on and I finally closed the curiosity forever. I can only attribute the strange longing for the sky to the genetic makeup of my body, not knowing my heritage. I have always had the strongest need to be around things and people that fly. It does not matter, model airplane, UFO, birds, full-scale airplanes, I am probably one of the few people in the world that goes nuts over a Frisbee or a kite. I later found out that none of my three half brothers were professional pilots, so I guess you could say, I am the lone eagle of my distant family.

Chapter One
Getting Started

When I was a kid, all I dreamed about was flying. I clipped newspaper articles and kept them in a scrapbook during the war. I had pictures of all the warplanes and I knew the names of the aces. Each new event in aviation demanded my attention. I loved every detail of flight and aviation. My father was involved in making parts for the war effort and delivered them to the Grand Central Airport in Glendale, California. I can remember the entire airport covered with camouflage and airplanes taking off and landing underneath fake houses with laundry hanging on clotheslines, it was all magic to me. I could hardly wait until I too would be a pilot. I built model airplanes of all types and sizes. In grammar school I built a model of Muroc Army Air Base complete with experimental aircraft and hangars. All my spare time was devoted to airplanes and flying, in class I would draw aircraft of all types and sizes. My English teacher asked me "don't you ever think about anything but airplanes?" I replied yes, but not for very long. She propositioned me that if I would read a book she suggested cover to cover, and write a report, she would give me an A grade. So I read "The Mayor of Castor Bridge by Thomas Hardy". It was the first book I can remember reading cover to cover. It was so good I couldn't put it down....I got an A. In my math class there were signs all around the chalk board, one read "the steam that blows the whistle, doesn't turn the wheels" and still another that said "time passes, will you?". In junior high school, there was a model shop and I immediately signed up only to find that the class was slanted towards model sailboats. I doggedly continued to build model airplanes but soon switched to boats because of the mentoring and close supervision of a really great teacher named Norman Hines. Mr. Hines patiently taught impatient young minds the value of craftsmanship and patience. His efforts were rewarded by his charges winning nearly all the first and second place trophies for racing and craftsmanship at the Echo Park Model Boat Races sponsored by the Los Angeles Evening Herald Express. I won a first place trophy and drill set with a small 13 inch boat on my first time out. I won a second place race trophy and a first place Craftsmanship award with a larger 39 inch boat. They were presented by a then unknown young actor by the name of Robert Mitchum. I also won a Ford Industrial Arts First Place Award, my boat was on display at the Ford Museum in Dearborn, Michigan. It later went to the Chicago Museum of Science and Industry, then back to the LA City Schools District offices. At the same time on weekends, I built contest free-flight models and went to contests, tagging along with anyone that would have me. During my trips, I set a couple of national records for free-flight models and began to design my own models for competition. I built u-control models that flew on wires, gliders of every shape and size. I liked scale models, if it didn't resemble a real airplane, I wasn't interested. I built several models of my own design. We flew all sizes and types of model airplanes at the school yard. Free flight and U-control. Mostly powered by small Cub, Baby Spitfire, K&B glow fuel engines. My Mom had several major operations. She eventually became the poster girl for Blue Shield Insurance Company. She wasn't home much and my Dad worked all the time so model airplanes became my baby sitter. When I was in school, I could be found working my paper route and working odd jobs to purchase hobby supplies and then rushing home to construct my next dream airplane. Just past my twelfth birthday, my Dad passed away suddenly. He was 44 he had worked hard all his life and he always encouraged me to build and fly models. He built a u-control model with a McCoy Red Head rear rotor 29. He bought me a Carl Goldberg Zing, a u-control model mostly made of slabs of balsa and a routed body which according to the box, used a .19 to .49 engine. Of course bigger was better so he bought the biggest motor a Madewell 49. Way overpowering the slender model airplane, we eventually flew it ever so briefly in the Rose Bowl Parking Lot. He was also proud of my sailboat trophies. It was shortly after that that I was flying one weekend at a contest and I lost sight of a model airplane when everyone else could see it plainly, in short, I needed glasses. I knew the legendary stories of the aces and I knew that they all possessed eagle sight, something I did not have. The handwriting was on the wall, my aviation career was doomed. I still loved aviation and still built and flew model airplanes. At the high school I attended, I enrolled in an aeronautics course. There was a link instrument trainer, we had to build a model airplane, and to top it off we were to fly in a real airplane and navigate one leg of a multi-leg flight. I still remember the exact moment when the wheels left the ground. We took off from the famous old airport, Grand Central in Glendale, California. I was in the left rear seat of a Cessna 170, and essentially, it was my aeronautical birth, I was smitten by the flying bug. I read every book or publication I could find on flying and aviation. I built and flew countless models of all shapes, sizes, and configurations. I had a favorite model of a Monogram Speedee-built Stearman biplane, that I would swing around on a string tied to a stick for hours on end, sometimes under street lights at night, taking off and landing over and over again. I belonged to model clubs and worked at the hobby shop after school. Most of my life would be spent working two or three jobs at the same time, never near full scale aircraft or the people that flew them. I read every paper, magazine, and book that had anything to do with aviation. It turns out that being smitten did not apply only to flying. After a high school football game there was a party. I took an attractive blonde with me, but she was not interested in me at all. While at the party, I noticed a noisy, lively, dark eyed, dark haired, slender beanpole of a girl attempting to be the life of the party and doing a pretty good job of it at that. I began scheming immediately and told the blonde I had to work early the next day and after I dropped her at her apartment, I raced back to the party only to find that someone else had taken her home. The next party I went stag and she was there. It did not take long before we were

14

in a dark corner on the couch steaming things up for all we were worth. I did not know her name but I took her home. We became high school sweethearts, went everywhere, and did everything together. We both wanted to go to college so we went our separate ways to different colleges and we only saw each other randomly. I did not think there was a future for me in flying so I turned to electronics the job of the future. Although when I entered college I was studying electronics, every chance I got I was up the hill at the airframe and power plant school longing and looking at airplanes in the process of restoration. After two years of electronics, I left the junior college and went to a state university to study aeronautical engineering. I thought now I was on track and heading towards my rendezvous with destiny. Engineering was tough for me I had learning disabilities and no matter how much effort I applied, I fell further and further behind. My counselor told me I was not cut out to be an engineer and I planned to join the Air Force in the fall; I wanted to be around aviation one way or another. During my stay at engineering school, I joined the flying club and soloed in a Piper J3 Cub. My instructor was very demanding and I realize now he probably saved my life several times over because of his strict discipline. He later became a very successful airline pilot. I once saw his picture on the cover of AOPA magazine, he was flying a Ford Tri-Motor for Scenic Airlines on furlough, so he finally got to fly an antique. For several days he told me he would not solo me unless I got him a ride in some antique airplanes at the place I worked on weekends at the Paso Robles airport. He soon tired of yelling at me and I soloed at San Luis Obispo, California's county airport. My first solo takeoff was uneventful but when I turned downwind at pattern altitude the realization struck me, I was alone and I was going to land by myself. The thrill of solo flight was overwhelming. I couldn't think about anything else, and my school studies suffered. The freedom of flight was a narcotic I never recovered from. I used to fly the little Cub over the ocean and watch the turtles and whales lazing in the ocean. A disaster occurred one foggy coastal day when a flying club airplane was scud running and hit a power line suspended invisibly above a highway they were following. The aircraft crashed in a deep ravine and a frantic phone call by one of the flying club members asked if I would go standby the wreckage until help came. The scene wasn't a recruiting poster for aviation. The poor fellow in the front was dead and the one in the back was moaning and I tried to comfort him but I knew he would not last until help came. It was a shock to my system to realize that flying could be fatal. I thought about flying and the danger and I decided it was worth the risk, at least for me. I spent many happy hours flying around the sand dunes on the beach, and just enjoying the sky. I hung around with pilots and the wannabees and all we talked about was flying, with little time given to school. I soon ran out of money for school and flying and my enlistment in the Air Force was due to take effect in August. I thought I would soon be around airplanes of all kinds. My wife to be and some friends took me to Union Station in LA and I soon was on my way to Lackland Airforce Base in San Antonio, Texas for basic training. On arrival, all of us had different clothing and so we were called "rainbows." We slept in the first morning, in the distance earlier we heard muted sounds, hut, hue, hree, hror, one, hut, hue,hree, hror, two without knowing what was going on outside the barracks. That day we were sent to the "green monster" a large warehouse type building where we got our heads shaved, vaccinated, and issued our clothing. The barbers sheared our hair like sheep, the medics stuck several needles at a time in our arms and dropped the empties in washtubs for disposal. We would step up to the station, told to look at the pinup on the post and wham, needles everywhere. The little guys went through without a hitch, the football jocks fell over before reaching the station and were lying about the floor like so much cord wood for later use, we just stepped over them. Further on we were asked our size for all sorts of garments, boots, and shoes, and eventually we got whatever they had. The next morning the muted sounds were explained. As

16

soon as reveille was sounded on and old record player, we fell out in formation for calisthenics in the street and counted cadence as we grunted and strained the baby fat off our unconditioned bodies. Soon we were marching in formation everywhere, smart stepping through the chow lines, and going to schools non-stop, and becoming however reluctantly, basic airmen. We completed basic and got our assignments to tech schools of all types. We were shipped off in a dilapidated old airliner with wires hanging out of the walls and nearly didn't get off the ground for starting troubles. Arriving in Biloxi, Mississippi, we were headed for school. They lost our basic training records enroute so we had to have all our shots over again, and of course we took basic training over again. Doing so we gained the name "Lowry boys", because we were originally sent to missle school at Lowry Air Force Base Denver. We were doing all sorts of menial jobs there when some one complained to their Congressman and next thing we knew we were on our way to radio and radar school, booted out of missle school before we saw one…. Next thing I knew I was marching and learning to become an airman and going to all manner of Air Force electronics schools, but the only airplanes around were on the other side of the base and I was nowhere near them. I had done pretty well and was in the top ten percent of my class. I planned to go on leave after school and marry my high school sweetheart. My mind was not on school and on my final exam I got a low grade on the practical test so it meant that I had to get a grade of 100% on the written exam so I could go home on leave and get married. I sweated bullets during the test, I changed several of the answers multiple times, I was sure I was not going to make it. When the results came, back I had scored 100% much to my surprise and I was on my way home to get married. My wife to be had all the preparations ready, we were married, honeymooned one night in Santa Barbara at the Al A Mar Motel,(it's still there) we packed a suitcase with an electric frying pan and headed back to Biloxi, Mississippi to finish my electronic schooling.

Chapter Two
A Different Direction

On the train to basic training, I had visions of fighters and bombers and me in the middle of them. The phrase "the needs of the Air Force comes first" was unknown to me but I found out they needed electronics people badly and not pilots wearing glasses so, I found myself attending USAF electronics school zipping through subjects in a few weeks that it had taken two years for college to complete. Selection of my lovely bride as a lifelong mate was a simple process. I asked the girls I dated if they would like to go fly model airplanes on Sunday morning, when they quit laughing I knew they weren't the one. One in particular not only didn't laugh; she asked what time I was going to pick her up. End of process. Well it really wasn't that simple but that explanation will do for the time being. Completing the Air Force school in air to ground radio, I was sent to an isolated radar site in Cottonwood, Idaho far from airports and any sign of an aircraft. I gained some rank and experience there and after about a year a friend was shipped out to Hopedale, Labrador. I opined that he got a rotten break and we had a send off party for him. A couple of weeks later I got orders to go to Cartwwright, Labrador about 150 miles south of Hopedale. I spent a year there…. One day on the way down the hill from the radar site   at Cottonwood Air Force Station, in Cottonwood, Idaho, a Stearman biplane flew over me and sprayed my car with pesticide. When I got home I told my wife," I am going to do that some day". In the year there, I gained a family member, my son Kevin. While still a baby, I left him with his mother and I was then shipped to my overseas assignment an isolated site near Cartwright, Labrador. My family stayed with family and I served a year on an isolated radar site far from any aircraft. I did get to ride a helicopter to the site, it was an old radial recip beast flown by a Canadian bush pilot, air force helicopters were restricted from flying to my new assignment because

18

so many had crashed in previous attempts. After an eight months tour of duty I returned to the states because of an award I won for performance, Best Airman 64th Air Division. I received two weeks in New York all expenses paid. My bride and I went to several Broadway shows and then she returned home and I had to return to the isolation of Labrador for another three months. When I left the states long skirts were in fashion and when I returned mini-skirts were everywhere, a great improvement in the world. When my wife picked me up at the airport, my son rode on my lap and stared at the stranger in a blue uniform, his face puzzled by the new guy in town. Not being the greatest parent to begin with I couldn't imagine what effect my absence for a year had on my son. We sort of grew up together. As the result of being the best airman in the 64th Air Division I got to choose my stateside assignment. I was headed for Beale Air Force Base, a SAC base in California and I thought at last I would be around aircraft. And around aircraft I was, I took care of the air to ground communication radios, the cable TV system, and the ham radio station, but none of my activities got me anywhere near an aircraft. I could see that I was getting nowhere fast and that the needs of our nation's air force and mine were not necessarily going to coincide. Although I was offered the opportunity to go to Officer Candidate School, I decided that a peacetime air force was not for me. In the specialty I served in, promotions were rare, if not frozen. On my return to civilian life I did what I had to do to take care of my family I got a job in electronics because that is all the work experience I had. Another great gift was added to our family, our daughter Rene. A fierce little bundle of lightning that illuminated our lives. She immediately wound her Dad around her little finger, moved right in on her older brother's territory, and made herself right at home. I was still looking up, I had soloed in college, but still a student pilot, I went from instructor to instructor as I moved, each time learning good and bad from an assortment of disinterested instructors building time for their future as airline pilots. I had now resigned myself

19

that flying was a hobby and so with a few dollars here and there I flew an hour now and then. With just a couple of hours to go till I could take my private check ride, my instructor was killed in a training accident. He was a great instructor and a good pilot flying a new type Cessna with a different airfoil wing and an all flying tail that was later modified for safety. They tried to land on a mountain strip, and midway down the runway after touchdown they realized they couldn't stop so they tried to go around and try another landing. In the process the terrain rose faster than the airplane and trying to avoid the trees the airplane stalled and crashed. All aboard were killed. Early on I discovered that death followed airplanes around with a disturbing frequency. Ignoring the danger, I found another instructor and I finally got my Private license. Now I could carry passengers for fun. My GI bill and the private license gained me entry to a commercial pilot training program. I worked for and got every license I could think of. I used money, barter, trade, and ended up with quite an assortment of licenses and experience. If I found an instructor with a rating I didn't have I traded him one of mine for his. Same with aircraft checkouts, If they needed someone to check out in a new type aircraft, I was their man. I began to flight instruct in my spare time and build hours logging as little as a few tenths in any aircraft I could gain the use of. I was still working in electronics and had worked my way up to Senior Member of the Technical Staff. My group designed and built prototype modems, teletype concentrators, and automated test equipment for satellite communications equipment. I made a trip and a presentation to Intelsat in Washington, DC and won a contract that was being contested by several large firms. Along with the title, I had a pocket full of pills so I could eat, sleep, and generally keep from falling apart. It was a dog eat dog environment that gnawed at me like a piranha past a hunger strike. I wanted out. The company I worked for provided the exit when I refused to sell an electronic device that did not meet spec to a trusting customer. They were upset because I would not lie to the customer and so when I returned from a business trip my pink slip and check were waiting and I was summarily booted out the front door after months of thankless overtime hours without pay. It was a humiliating experience being handed a box with the contents of my desk and escorted out the door so I could not even say goodbye to associates and friends after months of diligent work. It was a learning experience, I learned that corporate greed is ruthless and the lawyers that ran the company would stop at nothing for a dollar. All I had now were a pocket full of ratings and no job. After airport bumming a few days, I began free lance flight instructing full time. Flying six and seven days a week I made less money that I did engineering and the future looked bleak but at least I was around airplanes and the people that worked and loved (or hated) them. More ratings more hours more experience. I applied for jobs with the fire department, the sheriff, the police, the border patrol, and others too numerous to mention but the result was the same. They would not accept a pilot wearing glasses. I was nearly legally blind without glasses and had a wavier to get my second class medical. I was instructing instrument ground school at the local college and I had set up a training program for high school students giving them their first ride in an airplane. I took any job I could find that would make money flying. One morning the office girl asked me if I could drop skydivers, I said sure can. (I had never done it before). So, she introduced me to a long haired, hippy looking fellow by the name of "teacher" and we soon had made arrangements to drop divers from a Cessna 182. It was an opening of a real estate development in the desert and the jumpers were going to jump into the development several times during the day. They also had smoke canisters taped to their coveralls. After several drops we called it a day and I told teacher," hey instead of a few seconds in the air I can teach you to fly and you can stay up for hours". I didn't think he would take me seriously, but the following week he showed up on the roster for flight lessons. He completed his training in a few months, and bought his own Taylorcraft and flew it to British Columbia from Van Nuys, CA solo and returned. Strangely some forty years later we are still good friends, both of us survived a hazardous avocation and vocation. "Teacher" has thousands of jumps and 60 hours of freefall time, jumping out of nearly every type of aircraft, in many countries, he has flown coast to coast in a J3 Cub and is still jumping out of perfectly good airplanes. He also was a great elementary school teacher and inspired many young souls to a better life. We are both amazed that we made it this far. I continued to instruct at one of the busiest airports in the country, until I read an ad in the trade paper looking for and engineer/pilot for company in Canada. When I read the ad it looked like someone had written it for me, so I sent a resume and remarked to a fellow pilot "I bet there will be over a thousand replies to that ad", there were in fact 1400 I found out later, and I got a call in the wee small hours of the morning asking if my wife and I could come to Toronto for a job interview. The short story is I got the job. I flew a light twin, engineered, and tried to sell process control equipment. I helped to design a combustion control system for the largest continuous copper smelter in the world. We lived in a little town about thirty miles north of Toronto named Newmarket. I flew a C55 Beechcraft Baron on business flights and engineered and sold process control equipment. I was sent to Analog and Digital process control school in Marshalltown, Iowa. I traveled a lot. It was not my idea of a job, little flying, and lots of paper work. Another round peg trying to pound into a square hole. After a year of engineering and sales, I was told that the airplane was to be discontinued and that flying in all kinds of ugly instrument weather carrying company and business people was a "fringe benefit" by the new young bull taking over the office. I wasn't expecting to be blindsided by this situation so I gave the owner notice that I was leaving and I dropped my keys in the office, put my family on an aircraft bound for the southwest, and headed for an uncertain future in Southern California. The day before departure, my wife got food poisoning, so I put the kids and the dog on the airliner and sent them to their grand parents. I holed up in a motel until she was able to travel then we went home to California. I didn't own a car, had no home, and very little money left after shipping my family home, we lost all our furniture and possessions except the clothing on our backs. I was delighted that the company would ship my entire household to Canada as a condition of my employment but I never thought to ask how I would get it all back home if my job ran out. It was a tough lesson to learn. By now I had a son, a daughter, and a dog and my wife insisted that they all be fed, clothed, and covered so we returned to the desert where we used to water ski and rented a shack on the river. In heavy brush, the tin shed was full of other occupants. Spiders and crawling critters of all sizes and shapes. We took cold showers until we discovered a water heater in a shed outside. I searched for jobs everywhere but I was told I would have to live there for a couple of years before anyone would hire me for any job. The first job I got was scraping roofs in July for a roofer. The large steel rakes used to remove the roofing burned your hands. Heated to a fiery temperature by the unrelenting desert sun, I was soon convinced that no aviation future was on a roof near me. Not much encouragement for an aviator. I got part time work instructing at the local airport. I taught ground school. I made the rounds of the airports and asked for a job crop dusting but I was told that the seats were held by old timers and the only way I would get a seat was for someone to die. The newspapers frequently had stories of some hapless pilot that died in the crash of a crop dusting airplane so I figured it was just a matter of time. The statistical life expectancy of a crop duster at that time was seven years. Since I had been told no male member of my birth mothers family had lived past the age of forty-four I figured that was just about right and I still had plenty of time since at the time I was 36. I had 3500 hours of flying time mostly instructing, and I had passed my apprentice ag pilot tests, and had several hundred hours as a tail dragger pilot, the type of aircraft used to crop dust. We were running out of money and ideas so out of a clear blue sky a friend that had worked for me in electronics engineering, called and asked if I would like to work on a project in Ramsey, New Jersey. I told him I wasn't interested in working in New Jersey but after a while he asked if his boss called, would I at least listen? He was a good friend and I thought I at least owed him that much. That night I thought of all kinds of unreasonable demands hoping he would decline me out of hand. The next day he called and I carefully recited my demands to which he replied, how soon can you be here? There, I would be designing satellite and associated test equipment for IntelSat. I accepted and soon was commuting back and forth to New Jersey from the desert cabin. I had purchased an old Cessna 150 that had been a trainer with thousands of hours on the airframe and I used it to commute from the desert to Phoenix for the airline ride to New Jersey. I would work four days spend a weekend there and then four more days then home for four days. While in New Jersey I managed to get my seaplane rating in the Hackensack River at the Little Ferry Seaplane Base. It was so much fun I couldn't wait to get down there after work. While there I met an owner of a trucking company, he owned a beautiful Cessna 140 on floats. We flew around the Statue of Liberty and up and down the river, dodging power lines and flying over a castle on an island in the middle of the river. In the post 911 era this freedom is no longer possible. I was able to launch and retrieve aircraft from a wooden ramp which extended into the river. They would wet it down with a hose and then the aircraft would slide down the ramp like a duck and enter the water. My young instructor had a thousand hours on floats and had never flown a landplane. I finished the job on time and budget and returned home to the family, once again looking for a flying job. I was offered a permanent job in New Jersey but I didn't feel comfortable in a place that was dangerous to go out on the streets at night. It seemed like a very long time but I finally landed a job as an aircraft mechanic at brand x crop-dusters. In your minds eye, try to imagine a junkyard of airplanes and farm equipment with a few Stearman biplanes sitting around with the most evil smells in attendance and the blistering desert heat fuming the whole mass. A dirt runway ran along a very deep irrigation drain. Junk cars were scattered around in no particular order and for no obvious reason. There was a large steel hangar with junk piled all around outside and inside aircraft parts and pieces hung from the rafters, walls, and stacked on the floor in unsightly heaps. Large wooden tables were covered with fabric, dope, and other covering supplies strewn about with reckless abandon. Tools, hoses, engines, and engine parts were everywhere. Add to this a resident family of birds, snakes, mice, scorpions, lizards, spiders, and a couple of gophers and you have a fair picture of the place I would call home for the next several months. I finally got what I was asking for, to be around airplanes, but this wasn't exactly the setting I had imagined in my fantasies. After working all day there, I began to smell worse than the airfield. There was one advantage to my peculiar odor, I noticed that when I went to get a haircut, the five people ahead of me soon left and I was number one in line. The barber needed the money so he never commented on my aroma. There is a peculiar odor associated with agricultural chemicals, and like Pavlov's famous dogs, I salivate at the smell of defoliant to this day. The boss referred to himself as "a dollar waiting on a dime", he being the dollar and of course yours truly was the lower denomination. I wrenched and painted, and welded and fixed and repaired. Mostly on pesticide covered and encrusted parts that were worn beyond recognition. After a while, I was told that if I could build up an ag airplane from parts laying about I could have an ag seat. So with great dedication and a new sense of mission I began to build MY airplane. Of course, no one told me at that time, that others had been made the same promise and had tried, failed, and left. Also omitted was the information that as I got each assembly cleaned, repaired, and painted, it didn't always make it to my airplane. When I left for the weekend if an airplane broke down, my fresh parts were used to fix the ailing aircraft and another junk part was put in place of my fresh part.

Monday morning I would start all over again. I was making no progress towards my dream but the airplanes kept flying and I was learning all about the crop dusting business. I would be so tired at the end of the day, working on airplanes and engines, loading and flagging, and anything else that needed to be done, that when I arrived at home (the shack) I would sit in "Old Blue" my old junk Dodge pickup and wait until I could get up enough steam to walk in and get cleaned up for dinner. It was a really tough job and I started to lose my focus in the rush of fatigue and the constant demands by my boss. The entire operation was a zoo of many types of people necessary to get the job done. Cowboy was an old timer that did welding on equipment. He rolled his own cigarettes, and talked with a drawl. He had been a tank mechanic with General Patton in Europe in WW2 and his stories about leaving radial engines hanging from trees all over the country were fascinating for me to listen to. Three men were loaders and flaggers and general workers their names were Smooth Mouth (no teeth), Pickle Face (bumps all over his face), and Catfish. (Mustache and wide smile). They were hard workers and reliable as the sun day and night. There was an assortment of women and girls one of which would drive the pickup and locate fields, check for problems (people, animals, standing water, or bees) and set the flaggers on the field. They were called chasers and were the supervisors of their group. They were people from all walks of life. Students, vets, housewives, and some just hiding out. Just across the street was a junk trailer village with all sorts of trailer trash and a section where ladies of the night plied their trade. I repaired several airplanes and rebuilt a couple of Stearman biplanes from the ground up. I learned to load and flag, it was after all a tough, demanding, dirty business. I was ready to give up when two things happened. The first was my eye appointment. I went to get a new set of frames with clear and dark lenses and the eye doc asked me "do you want 20-20 or best correctable?" I hadn't heard that before so I asked incredulously," do you mean I could have better than 20-

26

20?". And he replied "yes but you may have headaches from eyestrain so I don't recommend it." I was elated, now I too could have eagle vision. headaches be damned.... I could see better than most people with normal vision. The second event was an accidental fire that erupted on the loading pit. The boss was severely burned while attempting to fuel the Stearman's center section fuel tank while standing on the biplane's hopper, the engine was idling and the tank ran over and down the trailing edge of the wing into the hot exhaust. I was working in the hangar when I heard a Whoosh, and a foreman John, said calmly, "fire". I grabbed a huge fire extinguisher and ran towards the burning biplane but the fire was so hot I couldn't get close enough to use it. The aircraft literally burst into flames, while the boss leaped from the airplane to the cement, the loader covered him with water from a load hose nearby. The fire from the plane was so hot that the taillight lenses fell out of a nearby truck from the extreme heat. I rushed him to the hospital in his pickup with the lights and horn on. Burn treatment was not advanced at the tiny hospital so I later had to take him out of town to a burn unit at a larger hospital a hundred miles away. I put a mattress in the back of my old Dodge station wagon and carried him to a metro hospital where he could get proper burn treatment. For several weeks I flew his wife to the hospital in a borrowed Bellanca. We were now short a pilot and I had been stashing my clean parts all over the place like a dog hiding his bones. In a few days, I had completely assembled my airplane except for the engine and the house rule was that no parts were to be taken from a complete airplane. In a short time, I had a fresh overhauled Pratt and Whitney 985 cubic inch 450 horsepower engine ready to install. I purchased my first of several crash helmets, I was going to kill bugs soon. There were several journeyman pilots around and they worked on commission so they weren't really happy about having to share with an apprentice. Dandy and I flew in the owners Piper Colt from our isolated area to where the Stearman resided below sea level in Brawley. I soon got checked out in a rental Stearman. It was beautiful. Painted in the old army training colors yellow and blue with red and white stripes on the rudder, and powered by a 220 Continental Radial Engine, a high time duster named Dandy checked me out. Dandy had a great smile and always looked like he had just raided the cookie jar. He loved the ladies and flew on his own terms. He and the boss were always at each other's throats over some problem or other. He spent his money as fast as he made it and managed to fly the rice country each spring to pay his bills and taxes. I was soon flying as an apprentice pilot. I got all the table scraps. The fields that were under power lines, the small fields, the triangles, and strips, everything that was just a few acres or difficult to fly, that was my lot. It was a huge challenge just to survive each job, each day, but I was flying, wearing coveralls, a helmet, earplugs, gloves and covered with oil and poison, I was flying. The boss insisted that we have our first load on before sunrise. The procedure was the same each day, get the maps, put the helmet, maps, windshield cleaner, rags, flashlight, and anything else needed in the cockpit. I had a hard time starting my airplane on the cold mornings. I noticed the old timers started them easily, so I crept around in the dark of morning one day and watched as the vet started his engine. He drank the last of his coffee, then looked around to see if anyone was looking, satisfied it was all clear he drained some fuel into his now empty coffee cup and tossed it on the outside of the exposed large air filter. He grabbed the propeller at the bottom and just walked away pulling and the engine started easily. (It worked for me too.) We didn't have electric starters so we would prime the engine, pull it through a few times, make the magnetos hot, and pull it through, and pretty soon chuff….. Chuff….clank….Clank and the mighty Pratt smoked and began to idle. We had to be careful on startups to not pump the throttle after the start. A huge fireball could erupt from the exhaust and set the poison covered fabric aircraft on fire. It would idle for fifteen minutes before the oil temperature was up enough to taxi. Our planes were under shades and the wheels were in ruts in the dirt that served as chocks so it took quite a bit of power to taxi out to get a load. They told me that if I wrecked in the first 500 hours I would not be able to get a seat anywhere, I was very careful. Brake adjustments were critical on the Stearman saddled with a large engine, because if they were too tight they would lock and roll the airplane on its back. Visibility was not a great feature of the Stearman duster. You sat in the back seat with the raised hopper in front and radial cylinders all around the outside. You pretty much learned to takeoff and land looking out the side much like Lindbergh and his famous monoplane. I knew that stall-spins were the nemesis of low time ag pilots so I fashioned a crude angle of attack indicator and mounted it on the left N strut. It helped me to visualize when I was going to get in trouble regardless of angle of bank or the load in the aircraft. It saved my bacon more than once. Along the way, I was learning. The first wire I clipped was a telephone wire. I saw it to late to pull up. I sailed through it like a knife through hot butter. The second was a power line. The boss had been riding me about how high I cleared the wires so one evening at dusk while I was starting a trim pass, I tipped a power line with my tail wheel and did not break the line but a rotten cross arm on a pole broke. A cast of thousands was called to repair the arm with the attendant expense. I had not hurt the airplane or me so I guess I was ahead at that point, but the owner wasn't pleased with the repair bill for the phone company entourage. One of the pilots was my mentor; he had over six thousand hours in the Stearman. One evening while we were flying together in a lettuce field he suddenly pulled up and headed for home, we had no radios so there was no explanation. I continued to spray with reckless abandon. I finally shut down the spray pump and headed for home. Now it was getting dark and when I arrived at the airstrip, I had no lights on the airplane and there were no lights on the strip except for one in the hangar window. Now my mentor's actions became clear, landing visibility was bad by day but at night without lights, landing a chunky biplane with little or no visibility forward was a

29

very chancy thing. I lined up with what I though was the runway end with only the light in the hangar window for a marker, I carefully felt for the ground skidding the tires on the runway and then carefully reducing the power. It was one of the best landings I ever made in a Stearman biplane. The incredible high-pressure grip my buttocks had on the upholstery on the seat probably contributed to the near perfect alignment with the runway and I taxied in without any problem. The next day I was sitting at the end of the strip with a load and ready to depart when my mentor landed and rolled maybe fifty yards. He then did a ninety-degree turn off the runway headed out through a furrowed cotton field, the plants flew everywhere, the sound of the engine surging and the sight of the biplane bouncing over the cotton furrows was far from my concept of reality. Suddenly the aircraft swapped ends and left the field back out on the runway. He hopped out and pulled off his helmet and looked at my astonished face and exclaimed, "Its all runway, just part of it is paved!" One day I watched as Dandy taxied out in the dry airplane. This is an airplane set up for dry materials with a large metal spreader under the belly. When he did the run up before takeoff, the engine barked and missed on one magneto. He tried to clear it several times with no luck, so he just took off anyway. The airplane barely cleared the ditch bank as he turned toward the field and I could see he was descending and making a forced landing with the now cranky engine bringing him back to earth. I jumped into a pick up truck and drove over to pick him up. As I walked up to the tattered old biplane he began to instruct me... "Now Ron if you land cross rows, hold the stick all the way back. It does two things, keeps the tail on the ground, and keeps your hands from shaking." More lessons...I was cleaning my airplane and a local colorful crop duster, a member of the competition, had obviously had to much to drink. He screeched to a halt in front of the hangar and slurred "are you gonna fly that thing?.... I explained that I intended to, soon, and he snarled out "man you got more guts than a slaughter house", he then observed that I was to small to do the job, climbed in the pickup and lurched down the highway. Today he is a well known and respected business man but you would never know it from his past. I guess you can always serve as a bad example. It was not long before I realized that there was more dirt than glory in the crop dusting business. I was tired of the constant maintenance, the dirty environment, and the little bit of work I managed to scrounge didn't pay much. It was a disappointment of major proportions. So reluctantly, I called a friend and arranged for a job interview for a job flying for a major electronics firm flight testing avionics. I didn't make it to the interview because I got a call from a crop dusting firm across town asking if I wanted to fly one of their new airplanes. In a small town everyone knows everyone's business, most of the gossip travels through the barber shop. They had heard I was leaving and needed a pilot. I thought what the heck, let's go see. The operation was spotless. The airplanes were spotless. I didn't have to wrench if I didn't want to. It was a first class operation, and I was hooked. I left Brand X dusters without breaking an airplane and gained a lot of valuable experience. I called and canceled the job at the electronics firm. When I first started the new job, I flew an older airplane but within months, I went to the Cessna factory and took delivery of a brand new Cessna Ag Wagon airplane and brought it home. We rode back to Wichita, Kansas in a light twin with the owner. We made a GCA approach to get through the overcast soup into the airport. When we arrived, people were waiting in the lounge. Judging from the conversations we had, they had been there quite a while due to weather. We were undaunted and began removing the spray booms and putting them inside the fuselage. We loaded up our stuff and one of the pilots asked incredulously if we were leaving and I replied in the affirmative. He had just bought a new Cessna 182 and asked if he could follow us west. So I told him stay close and don't run into us on the way out. The owner taxied out with a special clearance and we followed him out to the runway like obedient ducks. When the tower cleared him for take off we followed. He went on instruments through the clouds, the last I saw of him was the wheels retracting and the aircraft vaporizing into the clouds, we remained below the overcast, two Ag Wagons and one 182. We continued to the edge of the control zone and located a water tank with the towns name on the side. The three planes turned to the west from our south heading with the wide-eyed 182 pilot in trail. In just a few miles, the haze lifted to unlimited visibility and the happy 182 pilot turned to his homeward heading. We had an alternator failure on the way home and had to stop and repair it in Holbrook, Arizona. It was a Sunday and a gent at the airport drove us into town to get the necessary part. We continued on home a flight of two new airplanes. A new airplane, new friends, a new job, a new beginning.... The owner of the company was a flamboyant, eager, good-looking, womanizer. Among his better talents he was a Cracker Jack pilot doing things and taking risks even staff pilots would walk away from, shaking their heads in disbelief. He ran a spotless operation and we had gobs of people. He was also a sky diver and when we got through with work, I would take a load of jumpers up for an early morning jump. We played every chance we got. There were people everywhere. Each pilot had a pickup, a person to drive it and four or more flaggers to flag the fields with. They would step off so many paces and wave the flag for each swath. At that time before so many regulations, the girls wore halters and short shorts. It was difficult to pay attention to the swath with all the lovely distraction stationed about the field. I had only flown a short time when I was asked to fly some evening work in preparation for the night work that would follow. It was difficult for me to imagine that people would crop dust (spray) at night. I thought that pilots that flew ag work at night must have special powers of perception to fly under and around wires and other airborne snags. I wasn't in the least interested in participating in airborne snag removal, and much less doing it in the dark. In the desert, the hot sun and high temperatures would evaporate the spray quickly; the ultraviolet rays of the sun also quickly destroyed the effectiveness of the spray. The bugs being pretty smart would go down low in the plant or in the ground until night and then come up to feed. Because chemicals were becoming very expensive night flying came into being. The ideal time was thought to be between ten PM and six AM. We of course flew outside these boundries when the volume of work demanded that we just get it done. We had lights on the wings for work, two facing forward and adjustable up and down. Because of the higher speeds on turbines, three or more lamps might be installed for work lights. Another pair of lights were fixed down at a steeper angle for the purpose of taxiing on the ground and identifying electric power lines on descent into the field, these are called wire or obstruction lights. Another pair of lights were mounted on each wing pointing outward about a forty-five degree angle and used for turn lights. The pilot would put the beam on the ground and use it for an attitude reference during a turn on a dark and moonless night. Some of the pickups had strobe lights or rotating blue beacons so we could identify our truck from the competition. Our pickups had narrow band FM radios which made the setup and status of the fields much easier between the pilots and crew. Flaggers would be stationed on the corners of the fields with flashlights. You could see the flashlights easily for six to eight miles so it was not difficult to line up for the first swath run. It worked well until the flagger went to sleep, the batteries burned out in the flashlight, or the flagger met up with a large rattlesnake, in which case the light was likely to move quickly and go out. We tried all sorts of methods to mark and light the swath, and the flying became harder and harder due to new regulations and faster airplanes. We had many parties thrown by the owner, good food and good flying, and the pay wasn't bad either. The owner threw a large party at a Mexican restaurant. We were all eating and drinking a lot as we had been advised that there wasn't much work the next day so it was party time. About ten in the evening someone came in with a message we were needed for frost patrol. We would fly slow with the flaps down to stir the air over citrus trees in danger of freezing or tomato plants. I drank lots of coffee and lay down on the office floor to await the 4:30 AM call. When the call came I found myself the possessor of a giant size hangover. When I pulled the crash helmet on it was too snug. In the turns my head began to swell and soon began pounding to get out of the now super confining helmet. I never drank again when I knew I was going to fly, which was nearly everyday. The company I worked for became large and soon I found my self bearing the title Arizona Operations Manager at an outlying airstrip. There were only three pilots and myself. One flew and maintained the helicopter, which was fine with me as I had no training or license for the copter. This was going to be different.

Chapter Three
Changes in the Wind

Now I was the boss. I had two pilots and myself to fly the fixed wing and helicopter aircraft at our airstrip. The previous boss had left to start his own operation. He had used the company's resources to get to know all the customers and then proceeded to take all the business we had. I tried my best to keep things running but I did not know the customers or the "bug men" the people hired to watch the fields and send the spray work to an applicator. The operation was a challenge for me trying to learn managing crews and pilots and doing all the administrative chores as well. One of the pilots was a "prima donna" pilot. He didn't mind flying, but if his machine broke, he didn't want to get his hands dirty and would not fly unless someone fixed his airplane, usually me. About the same time, the owner sent me a new employee to build some trucks. We needed a small stake bed truck to haul chemical. Pumps and motors were mounted to mix and load the chemical. The new guy "Bob" could weld or build anything. He had been in farming for many years and attended the same university except he was in agriculture and I was in aero engineering. I was told to give him a couple of fields now and then to keep him interested, to dangle the carrot of the possibility of a flying job. A few weeks went by and one day the "Prima Donna" didn't want to come in for work because there wasn't enough work to please him. I told "Bob" to get his helmet and follow me. Soon the acres of work were pouring in and Bob and I were working our brains out. Bob was a low time pilot but when he flew, he was better than most of the journeymen I had flown with. We became a great team and the amount of work we could do was amazing. I was having marital problems and I had moved to the little town near the airstrip pending a divorce. I was putting in countless hours away from home and though I was providing for my family, I didn't see much of them. The old Cowboy told me once, "Ron ya better go home and see the missus or there's gonna be a lotta sad singin and slow ridin". Standing in front of a judge and declaring that I was a failure for the divorce proceedings sank my spirits to a new low. I spent a lot of hours trying to make the operation go but nothing I could do would undo the grip the previous boss had on the customers. The business began a descending spiral. It was winter and the high compression engines and thick oil made starting difficult some times. I climbed in one morning and began the start procedure so I could go out and do a small job. The battery would not turn the prop through. Standard procedure was to turn the mags off and open the throttle then pull the prop through a few blades then try a restart. When I pulled the prop through the first time the engine caught and since I had untied it from the tie downs it now began to accelerate at a fierce rate. I nearly got chopped to bits and I dove under the spray booms and attempted to catch it but it was too late. The aircraft did a dying chicken act and hit a building and ended up in a ditch next to the airstrip. I was not hurt but my morale sunk to a new low. As a flight instructor I had taught students to tie down the airplane, chock it, turn the fuel off and observe other safety precautions for hand propping an engine. But I wasn't propping it to start it, I was just pulling it through. I received a good lesson on how impulse coupled magnetos work, they work really well... especially if one of the P leads is broken.. How many times have you seen or heard some pilot or mechanic say "I was just pulling it through?". When I see people pulling an airplane by it's propeller I think, you're just one click away from eternity. The accident served me well I never repeated that trick again. The lesson nearly cost me my life. Later that week the man that gave me my start in ag flying was spraying a lettuce field and in a turn he was too low and caught a wing tip which caused the Stearman biplane to cartwheel and burn. He was killed instantly. He was an army officer in WWII and flew gliders into Germany. He had thousands of hours day and night ag flying and ran a crop dusting service that employed a lot of people in a poor area. He always gave

36

one hundred percent. He again reminded me that this is a dangerous business, if you make a mistake you pay with your life. At my new job things were getting so slow that we didn't have much work and the owner finally decided to sell the assets of the remote operation and called me back to the home base. The helicopter guy stayed and ran an operation there for many years. Years later, I got my helicopter rating and flew ag work for him. I was glad to be just an employee with no responsibility except to fly my daily work. Things were going well for a while and even "Bob" had returned and was my flying partner. We had six pilots and Bob and I did three fourths of the work. We just plain loved to fly and be as efficient as we could. If I trimmed the north side he got the south. We always positioned ourselves opposite each other in a field so there was no danger of a collision. We didn't trim in front of each other causing spray to cover the others windshield. Our turns were tighter and faster than the others. If something broke, needed adjusting, or if chemicals needed mixing to keep up we did it without hesitation. It was too good to be true and we were getting paid for it. All good things come to an end and so it was with the operation we were in. The owner decided to go to helicopters and he and one of the employees got their ratings. He notified us that the fixed wings were being closed down and we would be unemployed soon. Our last big job was several miles away and we took five airplanes and two trucks to the job. We parked a truck at each end of the airstrip and three airplanes operated off one end and two off the other in opposition. We had to sequence take offs and landings but it was great fun. When you had your load you turned on your work lights to let the other aircraft know that you were ready and he would give way. We would blast off in a cloud of dirt and a hearty "HI YO Silver". When we finished, we flew in formation back to base. It was the last of the ideal operation but it sure was fun. I was now faced with the loss of my job and now had another family member to care for close by, my Mom. My stepfather, who had served under Eisenhower in Europe, and worked many years for retirement, had sold the home I was raised in and my folks were preparing to retire to the much loved river cabin they had prepared. In an uncharacteristic move, he asked that I take him for a ride in my airplane up and down the river. He hadn't flown before and never asked me before. In flight, he said "if there is something you want to do you had better do it now, you won't live forever". I flew him up and down the river and he seemed to really enjoy it. It was to be his only airplane ride. They went home to close the house and move on to retirement. While my Mom was changing to make the trip to the river she heard my stepfather say "Oh Oh Mom" and he hit the floor with a thud. The medics were summoned but he was dead on arrival at the hospital. Another page in my book of life had turned. My future was uncertain and I had a lot of responsibility. I looked around and tried to think of something to do so I wouldn't have to move and upset our now comfortable life.

Chapter Four
A New Beginning

The fixed wing pilots were now faced with the prospect of finding a new job which meant moving. Partner Bob and I were not happy about moving so I asked if he was interested in a partnership. It didn't take long before we were rolling down the runway in my old Swift. The Swift was built in 1946 by people that built fighters for WW2. It had 145 horsepower and hydraulic retracted landing gear. The load of two people and full fuel made the pre-dawn takeoff ponderous. We were headed towards a major airport for an airline ride to a dealer for the prospective purchase of an ag airplane in Hayti, Missouri. We deliberated a long time on which would be the safest airplane with which to begin our career as ag pilots, but all said and done the only one we could afford was a Grumman Ag Cat A large mostly metal biplane that looked like the aeronautical equivalent of a bumble-bee. Powered by a Pratt and Whitney 985 cubic inch 450 horsepower engine it was a genuine workhorse. We went to Missouri to pick up the airplanes for the ferry flight back to the desert. Neither one of us had ever flown an Ag Cat so the excitement of the departure was pretty high. Right off the bat I got lost. Yep, that's what I said. The Commercial Pilot, Instructor, hero ag pilot had mistaken a triangular airport on the early part of our flight for another nearby and assumed it was the correct check point. At least we were flying west all the time so we weren't far off course. We stopped to ask directions at the next airport and soon got on track. When we got as far as Albuquerque, the weather got bad and we were flying under snow flurries. Bob was used to flying fuel injected airplanes and wasn't used to using carburetor heat in the desert. His engine nearly failed until he located the carburetor heat control. A few backfires later the engine resumed running smoothly. We waited on the weather and finally got a break so we piled in and headed west. A few miles west a wall of clouds was before us and I spotted a hole and proceeded to head for it. When I cleared the other side I looked back in horror, Bob was nowhere to be found. Understand that his fiancé was waiting back home to go to Hawaii to get married. I thought, "man am I going to have a lot of explaining to do". I circled up to gain altitude to clear the low lying clouds, once above them I could see Bob circling around on the other side. I descended through the broken clouds, waggled my wings and off we went westward. The ceilings kept lowering on our trip and finally at Gallup, New Mexico in heavy rain I spotted the airstrip near the highway and we landed. After taxiing in, a car raced to our tie down area. I thought we were going to get busted but, an enthusiastic fan emerged from the car and exclaimed "I knew those were biplanes, I saw you coming in". We flew into another snowstorm after leaving Winslow, AZ. westbound. I kept an eye on Bob and soon he disappeared into the white of the snow. I went as far as I dared and then did a 180 degree turn and headed back to the departure airport. Bob also made the same decision. We both continued on for a while then returned to the airport and spent another night at the motel. When we left in the morning the airport people told us to look for downed aircraft in the mountains. Two had been lost during the night. We didn't see any on the trip and everything was covered with snow. On arrival at home, our normally clear airport was in process of hosting a sand storm to celebrate our arrival. We circled around and located some landmarks and landed. On a handshake we had a place to park our airplanes on a old WW2 cement slab. Okie Grower had a lease on several hundred acres on an old B24/17 transition base. He had planted several 200 acre pivots of alfalfa and we made a deal to park our planes for a discount on his spray bill. A big man, he had bright red hair and arms as big as most mens legs. He was a working dynamo. He could pick up a bale of hay and throw it in the back of his pickup without so much as a grunt. Okie was one of several children born to a poor family on a farm. So poor in fact, his parents gave him away to a neighboring farm to work for his keep at the age of eight years. Even as an adult, he used to call his "mom" once every week without fail…She had raised him from a boy and he considered her his real mom…Okie had been married several times, and one day he said if a strange woman shows up, tell her I left weeks ago. He was always coming and going at all hours of the day and night for a rendezvous with some willing lass. He flew a Cessna 182 and one night he tried to land on the strip where we worked. We had left a fertilizer tender parked on the runway thinking the vendor would pick it up at sundown. The vendor did not. He narrowly missed plowing into the tender and chewed us out for leaving it there. We didn't do that again. His most recent divorcee showed up one day and she seemed to take it all in stride. Star, A beautiful, statuesque, blonde, had a great sense of humor and was liked by all. Okie began to cohabit with her on a regular basis. Okie also had a young man Burt, that was his protégé. He worked the kid like a slave, but in return, he paid him well bought him motorcycles and trucks, and taught him the hay business from the ground up. Years went by and Okie prospered and expanded while we operated our ag airplanes from his slabs. He moved to a town a couple of hours away and continued to run the hay operation from afar with his adopted protégé. We were so busy, we didn't notice that Okie was missing for a couple of months. He was so secretive that we thought nothing of it. His pickup turned up in Mexico with blood under the rubber mat in the back….The bodies weren't found for a long time. One day, the new lease holder decided to expand the pivots. As the tractors neared the burial spot, the killer decided to have a friend help move the bodies so they wouldn't be found. The friend decided he wasn't going to be involved so he called the police. Burt, the protégé, had killed both Okie and Star and dumped their bodies in a pit near an old fifty caliber firing range. Things began to happen. A lot had to happen in three months. We had to pick up the airplanes and ferry them back, then set up the spray system for the area. We built a couple of load and service trucks, and set up the office for business including all the licenses and permits. Agricultural

41

aircraft are set up to spray or put out dry material with attachments to the airframe. The hopper is a tank made of fiberglass and it usually has a baffle to stop the liquid from shifting around and causing the center of gravity to shift and cause difficulty in controlling the aircraft. At the bottom of the hopper, a gate is hooked to a handle in the cockpit. This allows the liquid load to be jettisoned in event of emergency. The same gate is used to allow dry material to be metered into a device known as a spreader. A spreader is an aluminum or stainless steel box attached to the bottom of the hopper with a triangular box with vanes curved to spread the seed or fertilizer to a wider swath. A wind driven fan turns a bar with tines which break up the chunks and keeps them from jamming in the bottom of the hopper. When liquid is used, the spreader is removed, and the wind driven spray fan and spray booms are attached for spraying. A handle in the cockpit turns the spray to the booms on and off, and a variable pitch fan assembly allows adjustment for different pressures. Some fans are cockpit adjustable and some are ground adjustable only. Spray nozzles are attached with small pipe fittings. They come in several configurations. Some nozzles have a swirl plate which spins the liquid followed by an orifice plate which controls the rate volume. Others have a rotating cap that shuts off or changes the orifice and the flow rate. Each nozzle has a shutoff assembly with a rubber diaphragm which opens under pressure and shuts off via spring cap pressure when the pressure is removed. Some nozzles have miniature propellers that spin a can with holes in it to atomize the spray. In practice small droplets are used for pesticide to get coverage under the leaves of plants and large droplets are used for herbicides to reduce drift. The smaller the droplet the more the drift. Occasionally there is a need to make the chemical last longer in the field. When vegetable oil is added to the mix and the chemical will last up to about two weeks. Adding the oil increases the drift to non target areas. By using a venturi in the spray valve a suction is created when the spray is shut off called "suck back". Suck back actually empties the boom and nozzles each time the handle is closed, this in theory and practice keeps the nozzles from dripping in turns A lot of time is spent calibrating and checking the spray pattern for optimum results and minimum drift to susceptible crops. We used a system called a smoker where oil is injected into the exhaust system on the engine which creates a dense smoke when a button is pushed on the control stick. If the pilot is spraying near a susceptible crop, he first lays a pass of smoke along the edge of the field to see if the smoke drifts to a dangerous area. If the smoke drifts towards the field in question, he doesn't spray, if it does not then he puts a few passes next to the field on the chance that the wind will shift. In extreme cases a pilot may have to wait several days to make the application under favorable conditions. This is a highly regulated business so there were at least 12 different government agencies involved not including insurance. Partner welded the trucks and I ran the parts and administrative duties. When it came time to give the business a name I wanted an acronym for speed so I wrote down the word FAST. I wanted to associate the company with the farm industry so I came up with Farmers Aerial Service Team, because we were in fact a team effort. In the middle of the following January the trucks were completed and the airplanes were ready. We flew our first loads in February. A load truck is a pretty versatile and complex piece of machinery. It consists several components. A mix tank for chemicals, an 8 horsepower motor, and the plumbing and valves which allows the tank to agitate the material or push it through a load hose to the airplane in a matter of a couple of minutes. Also on board is a fresh water tank of about a thousand gallons, it can be filled by another pump of five horsepower or more from a sand point, canal, or other water source. Another 500-gallon tank is for avgas and of course, there is another small pump for that purpose. Add hoses, couplers, night-lights, business radio, and storage space for chemical and you have what is commonly known as a load truck. The truck can be a two and a half ton vehicle or many other configurations including a pickup pulling a trailer, and is used to service the aircraft. In California, they are called instruments of animal husbandry by the Highway Patrol. When fully loaded with chemical, avgas, water, and equipment the beast requires a careful driver and operator. The truck is operated off of dirt strips where mud and sand exist and other hazards to moving and using the truck. If the truck is disabled or if any of the systems are inoperative the entire operation comes to a screeching halt. Of course there are variations of sizes and shapes but basically all serve the same purpose. All this equipment is needed because we did not do much crop dusting we did crop spraying, most of our work was wet. We had one boom truck, which was a hydraulically operated bucket that would hold a ton or more of dry material. The bucket was raised up and over the hopper lid opening of the aircraft, a cloth sock was inserted in the hopper and a gate tripped, allowing the dry material to funnel into the hopper. In the priority of things to do, the aircraft are repaired and readied first because that is where the income comes from. Next the mix trucks, and finally the pickups used for the purpose of scouting the fields. When mid February arrived we started work, and work we did. We sprayed day and night. The two of us were like a well-oiled machine soon honed into doing the work of three. When flying was done we worked on broken trucks or talked to farmers, or paid bills or talked to county officials it was a seven day a week job and nearly 24 hours a day. We soon began a spilt workday where we would get up and fly in the dark early morning till ten am then worked on repairs until noon then lunch and then a nap. Then back in at four in the evening to map and set up crews and finally back in the cockpit at seven pm then fly till work was done, at midnight or later then repeat the process next day. We loved to fly and lived to do it. Along the way, several things happened to complicate things. The first year we made 7500 dollars a piece and paid all our bills, we made a lot of money but the expenses ate it up, parts, crew salaries, gobs of insurance, equipment and of course lots of avgas. On one evening when I came in for a landing, I noticed our loader had a spot of chemical on his pants. Since we were using a particularly nasty chemical I told him to take off his pants, wash, and put on clean coveralls, then I left. On the next landing, he was wearing coveralls and I thought there was no problem. I got a radio call that he was very sick and when I landed, I found he had pulled the coveralls on over his jeans! We rushed him to the hospital and he soon lapsed into a coma for about 6 hours and then recovered. It was a close call. We nearly lost one of our most valuable employees. We clipped a couple of power lines on the way but other wise we were extremely lucky. We were going great guns until the next year in the month of August. In the desert there are monsoon like thunderstorms usually at night during the summer. We had a lot of work to do and so we worked later than usual trying to get the work done before the inbound thunderstorms arrived. In each turn, we would look toward town and look for signs of haze. If the lights looked blurry, we would radio each other and make a mad dash for the airstrip. Sometimes there was not time to return to base, so we would land on a road and park behind some hay bales to weather the storm. One night when we had landed, the competition's pickup appeared and the chaser was looking for their pilot and plane. He had landed on the median strip between the freeway lanes in almost zero visibility. One night we ran out of luck. We had radios to the trucks and while I was working down south of our airstrip, I saw a bright flash, much like lightning, and then an instant later I heard the gasp and cry of one of our dearest lady flaggers. I knew without a word what had happened. My partner had hit a power line and crashed on the first swath run through the field. He of course had a full load of fuel and a full load of chemical. He hit a couple of twelve thousand volt lines and the flash blinded him. He knew by the feeling in the seat of his pants the airplane was slowing so he kept pushing forward on the stick to keep speed up and dove into the ground with the prop hub and landing gear hitting the ground nearly simultaneously. He didn't have his chin strap buttoned so

45

his helmet came off and went through the windshield. He was hurt pretty badly and luckily the the fuel went into the crater and the hopper burst and the chemical went in the hole behind the gas so there was no fire even though the exhaust pipes were cherry red on impact. I immediately called the loader to head the mix truck over to the crash site and directed him to set up the water hose in case of fire. My daughter was flagging on the same truck and because she didn't know which airplane was working (they looked identical) she ran to the crash site expecting to see me and instead saw Bob. She and the loader released his safety belt and pulled him out of the aircraft(we weren't sure it wouldn't catch on fire) and drug him away from the aircraft while I landed at a local strip and called the ambulance. I still marvel that the two lightweight kids were able to haul the over two hundred pound pilot out of the airplane. He had broken collar bones, and various cuts and bruises, and considering the ride, it was a miracle he was still living. The aircraft was totaled, it had hit on the landing gear and propeller shaft making a huge crater in the soft plowed ground. The spray pump mounted between the main landing gear was never found, disappearing in the soft dirt somewhere below the wreckage. When I landed at a competitor's airstrip for help, the lights were out because of the crash and I nearly ran over a helicopter sled parked on the runway in the darkness. The next few hours were spent running to the hospital and the crash site trying to get the disabled aircraft taken apart and removed from the field and trying to get partner air lifted to a bigger hospital. The insurance adjuster looked over the wreckage and commented that he had never heard of anyone surviving a crash of that magnitude, there wasn't much left of the twisted Ag Cat. Now I was confronted with doing the work of three airplanes with one pilot. I learned a valuable lesson about human nature. None of the growers was concerned with how partner was doing they just wanted their fields sprayed. I worked long hours but in the end, they took their work to the competition on the promise of sooner application. My world was turning upside down and I tried to hire another pilot but finding a pilot that was capable of doing the work and flying at night was a great risk. If we lost another airplane or injured another pilot, it didn't seem worth the risk. I plugged on and at the end of the season, my partner said he didn't want to fly any more. I didn't want a partner that didn't fly so we agreed to split the partnership. I sold my interest and partner continued to operate the business with hired pilots. In one night, my dream of owning my own successful business ended and I was out of work. It seemed like the end of the world. Another bend in the road appeared. One of the mechanics that worked at the airport had started his own business building up helicopters for the tuna fleet in San Diego. Since I was looking for work he invited me to be the avionics manager for the hangar. I was living in my travel trailer and working on the avionics for the helicopters used on tuna boats for fish spotting. There was a bright side, I bought a twenty five foot sailboat that needed work and I started sailing. I figured that sailing was like flying and I needed good instruction. I hired an old salt seaman to instruct me and my family on the finer points of sailing. After an hour of complex sea terminology and confusion we docked. I paid the fee for the instruction. After the old salt left, I told my family, now let's go out and figure this out for ourselves. We did and it turned out to be lot of fun and relaxation which lasted for years. I already had an old D model Bonanza, and I picked up an old Porsche that had wiring problems and got the whole mess running at once. Software, one of the kids I was teaching to fly said, "Ron you're the only guy I know that has won the triple crown." I hadn't really thought about it that way, but they were all dreams of mine at one time or another. I had hopes that I would get to test fly some of the choppers but it wasn't to be. I spent long hours wiring, documenting, and installing avionics in an assortment of helicopters. I wasn't flying much except to commute to the town where we were renting our home. Along with work I was studying and getting ready to take the FAA Airframe and Power plant Mechanic License tests. I passed. I spent a lot of time sailing and hanging out at the docks on weekends. The rest of the time I worked without watching the clock on a variety of strange projects. One of which was a VHF direction finder which was used on boats. I figured out a way to modify it so that the antennas stuck out from the bottom chin of the helicopter. Nearly all the antennas were on the bottom since there were few acceptable places on top. It worked great and was done in great secrecy. While it was still concealed in the hangar I got a phone call from one of the boat captains and he wanted one of the DF's like so and so has. It turned out they talked on the radios at sea more than I thought. I went to Panama a few times to repair radios and electrical systems. On the way back to Miami I rode with one of the mechanics that used to work airlines. As we taxied in he said "we're going to the revetment". Curious I asked, "what for?". His answer was "in case the bomb goes off it won't hit the other aircraft". We left and the bomb squad went aboard with a dog. It didn't blow. Flying can be dangerous in ways I never considered.

Chapter Five
Whirly Birds

My new job was to be an avionics manager. My job was to install complex switching and power for the many radios and other avionic gadgets for helicopters used by the tuna fleet searching for tuna all over the world... The helicopters were used to scout for tuna marking their presence with a low frequency transmitter installed in a float that could be tossed out in a school of tuna as the helicopter flew over. It was used for a beacon so the ships could come and home in on the schools of tuna. There were many long hours spent making wire looms, documenting the wiring, and making sheet metal panels for the many controls and switches. I didn't get any helicopter time so I enrolled at a school and began flying the whirly birds in my carefully rationed spare time. The little Hughes helicopter looked like a bug. It would barely hover with two people inside on a hot day. It had some nasty tendencies if you weren't careful in it's operation. A collapsed landing strut could destroy the entire helicopter if landed hard on the skid. Autorotations were very nearly the wildest thrill ride I ever experienced. I never realized how dangerous it was till I witnessed a student at Deer Valley airport doing an autorotation in the little Hughes helicopter. It looked like it was pushed off a tall building and fell straight down like a rock. Suddenly stopped, flared, and touched down like a feather. It was a demanding trainer and I soon mastered the fundamentals and began building time in the hills around San Diego. I took off and landed on every place and situation I could find. I practiced emergency procedures in the washes around the Del Mar Race track, which included a flight over the water near Black's beach. (a clothing optional beach). Soon I had the much coveted helicopter rating. It was so expensive to fly that as soon as I had the rating my flying stopped for the lack of money. The job took more and more of my time with more complex installations. Soon I was asked to go to Panama to do repairs on choppers that had been worked on by unskilled people. There was no promotion, no money, and the work and travel was tiring beyond belief so I gave notice and now I was another unemployed pilot. I had picked up my airframe and power plant mechanic rating along with the helicopter ticket. I was out of work for several months and as the money ran out the IRS was threatening me almost daily for tax money from the sale of the business and other income. We were very close to losing our home and most of what little income I had. I was out banging on doors and chasing an ag seat. One operation I walked into needed a pilot to fly a 450 Stearman biplane putting out sulphur dust on sugar beets. The Stearman was a fire trap.The sulphur was electrically charged to make it stick to the plants which made it more likely to catch fire, and to make things even worse the Stearman had a hard canopy that pivoted up and down over the cockpit so that in a roll over you wouldn't be able to get out. But I needed the money and this was a flying job. I flew sun up to sun down putting out thousands of bags of sulfur. Multiple sets of semi double flat trailers would appear each time I emptied them. At the end of a days work the loaders looked like honey bees coated with yellow pollen. When the loaders loaded the sulfur they put a pair of coveralls over the front of the canopy to keep the dust out of the cockpit but it only made things worse. When I applied the throttle the dust trapped at the junction of the canopy and fuselage was blown into my eyes. The pain and watering of my eyes was so bad that at times I would climb up and close my eyes, hold the stick between my knees and wait till the dust cleared enough for me to see. Goggles did no good, nor did splashing milk in my eyes at the end of the day help the discomfort. I flew sulfur for nearly five months non stop. In time the lead pilot quit and I got to transition to a turbine which was one of my goals. The speed was great and the maneuverability was better than I had imagined. We were knocking out huge blocks of acres each night. I made the transition without incident until one night I took off and headed for a field in the distance. When I got to the field the strainer clogged up on the first pass so I had to return to the strip I was working off. Now two things conspired to put me in harms way. The first was the fact that the wind had shifted so that there was a slight quartering tailwind. The second was that the turbine engine took a long time to spool up from flight idle and I had carefully pulled the throttle all the way back to make sure I didn't overshoot the landing since I also had a heavy load to land with. About halfway down the runway I realized the airplane wasn't going to stop in time so I applied full power. I pushed the throttle wide open but nothing happened. The turbine wouldn't spool up in time to make the go-around (I thought) and a crash was imminent as my load truck was parked at the end of the runway.   Also at the end on the other side was a stack of hay bales some 10 or 12 feet high. Resigned to the crash I braced myself and just before impact the turbine whooshed to life and dragging the right wing knocking off nozzles as I went, the left wing got enough lift to clear the hay bales.   Miraculously the aircraft lifted off and I returned for an uneventful landing without a few nozzles and a dinged aileron. My loader summed it up nicely, " man that was intense". I patched up the airplane and put some more learning in my kit bag. In the area where I flew, fog was known to come in without warning and we were cautioned that several locals had died trapped in instrument weather without the instruments for such weather. I was nearly trapped by low visibility one night near the Salton Sea. It was lucky I noticed the halos around the navigation lights in time. I finished the field in incredible low visibility and returned to the airstrip and landed. We waited till the fog lifted and then went back to work. There was a lot of activity at night near the border so caution was the watchword. I loaded at a strip right near the border and I could see illegals crawling under the fence and walking by the airplane narrowly missing the whirling propeller. On one ferry flight, a Learjet cruised by me headed south about a hundred feet above the ground with no lights visible. On another occasion, at a remote strip near the border. I would get bored and did not turn on my landing lights till the last minute just to see how far off the center line of the unlighted runway I would be, when I turned on the lights, two helicopters, and a couple of light twin engine aircraft scattered thinking I was the law, making a drug bust. I made enough money to pay my taxes and bills and the relationship between me and my then boss was strained over some disagreements in procedure. There was no chance that I would be allowed to fly the only turbine helicopter operated by the company. I began looking. I got an offer to fly ag in a helicopter. "Boboso", owner-operator of the operation I had once run, had an opening, so I started fixing trucks and flying helicopters.

The helicopter I was to fly was like the type seen on "MASH". It carried only a small 65-gallon load in two saddle tanks mounted on the skids. It flew at a painfully slow 65 miles per hour. We took off and landed on specially prepared trucks with a platform on top with hydraulic operated wings that made the platform about 12 by 12 feet. We were on and off the truck about every six minutes so we got lots of practice at taking off and landing on top of the truck. There were hazards, especially at night. If the wind shifted while you were gone with a load so that you weren't landing into the wind, it was easy to overshoot and clobber the tail rotor. On takeoffs if the engine sagged or you had insufficient rpm's the tail rotor could hit the truck when you leaped off the side. When we shut down for the day we carefully watched and listened as the bird spun down. We were looking for bad bearings, creaks and groans indicating something was broken or bent. We would touch the bearing hangars to see if they were hot. Preflight was careful and we carried a grease gun along and carefully greased everything. It was said that if there was no grease or oil falling off the airframe, then it was out of grease and oil. One day when I landed, I noticed that the back half of a bolt with the nut and cotter pin was gone. Only the front half remained. This bolt was located in the pitch link a control which made the main rotor blade change angle. My hair stood on end when I saw it. We had bought some bogus bolts without knowing, from a reputable supplier. Later, bolts had part numbers

52

and were tested and marked with an attendant increase in price maybe 5 times. Flying the chopper at night was a real challenge especially if the wind was blowing If no grass or weed was visible on bare ground, pedal turns of 180 degrees could be disorienting so we tended to fly around the turns more which increased safety because of the extra speed. Low altitude and low speed are deadly in any helicopter while maneuvering. The area of the chart that shows dangerous speed and altitude is called the "dead man's curve". I piled up hours and got pretty relaxed most of the time until one night approaching the truck I had a tail rotor failure. The truck was parked near some power lines so I pulled on the collective and banked away from the truck spinning like a carousel. Using the spinning lights for a horizon, I timed the descent and control positions so that I hit flat and the only damage was bent skids, my ego, and my spine. I didn't know I was hurt so I didn't go to the doctor. About a week later my back began to hurt. The seat was made from large rubber bands cut from an old inner tube. When I hit the ground the bands flexed down and I hit the company radio mounted under the seat which stopped my downward progress rather suddenly. The result was an injury which still plagues me to this day and the only time in my entire career of flying when I was injured. This was going to be harder than I thought. I fixed the bird and became a little more careful about truck position next time. On another flight as I was turning into the field for the next pass the engine began to lose power and I had to autorotate down nearly missing the power lines on the edge of the field. Working a helicopter is deadly serious business with no room for error. Playing with one is a different story all together. We were headed to work late one morning and as I crossed a country road, I spotted an ice cream truck in the middle of nowhere. I landed on the road, locked the collective and cyclic, and left the helicopter running on the road, and proceeded to buy an ice cream. My loaders showed up with the mix truck and soon were slurping the ice cream too. My boss showed up next and landed next to me. And you guessed it his load truck showed up too. What a sight, trucks, people, helicopters, and an ice cream truck in the middle of the desert. What a great way to start the day. Some times my load truck would stop at the store for food or a soda and while I was waiting I would land in an open hay field and watch the animals or stars until the load truck came and parked for the next job. I always hope a UFO or some interplanetary being would show up where no one but me could see them, but it never happened. I liked spraying with a helicopter we never did dry work like the fixed wings did. We did use Pheromone pods which spun little fibers of sex hormone which stuck to the plant with a sticky goo. It supposedly confused the male moths so they couldn't find the female moth and thus reduce the population. It made the helicopter a sticky gooey mess which was very hard to clean and even more difficult to maintain. The pods were very heavy and used a lot of electricity. I was always taught to maintain the engine rpms carefully without over speeding the engine. That nearly caused me to crash a couple of times. Then one day while talking with an old timer he said "you aren't using enough rpm's on takeoff, it's going to get you in trouble. He cautioned me to use max rpm then add 50 rpm for mom, 25 for each of the kids, and ten for the dog and then pull collective." You know it really worked great for me, I should have done that earlier. I had several near misses and mechanical failures were piling up with all to familiar frequency. I decided it was time to change direction. I was going to quit my job and travel. We sold our house and got a travel trailer and were living on the river in a trailer camp in readiness for our departure. About that time partner Bob showed up and offered a job flying. Although I was a previous owner and partner I started at the bottom again as a staff pilot. I flew the smaller Cessna Ag-truck (basically a powered glider) while the other journeymen flew the larger Air Tractor with a 600 horsepower nine cylinder radial engine. I flew two loads for every one the tractor carried so I worked twice as hard as the others for the same money as we split the monthly gross. Of course I got all

54

the small loads and wired fields in the interest of safety and efficiency. It was fortunate that a lot of work came in and I stayed very busy. It wasn't long before I was transitioned to the larger airplane. It carried twice as much but took a lot more effort to fly so I was more tired that ever. I now had gained an inspection authorization which allowed me to sign off aircraft for their airworthiness inspection, and major repairs as needed. Another pilot, Buck was an ex Vietnam helicopter pilot. He was an expert mechanic and a gifted pilot. He was also angry most of the time about his experiences in Vietnam. I worked long hours beside him and soon came to know of his terrible experience in Southeast Asia. I tried to humor him into a better mood but it only worsened his attitude so I just kept quiet most of the time which, made him even angrier. I began to read everything I could find on the Vietnam War in an effort to understand his moods. Soon my self-education directed me to remain silent lest I waken the terror that was his. He carried a belligerent attitude that made me vigilant while working around him. It was as though provoking a dangerous situation made him feel better. One day while waiting for the load truck to arrive he said, "We shouldn't be breathing this chemical it isn't good for us", my reply was" the crash is going to kill you". We were close friends for several years, until one day a maintenance disagreement separated us. He no longer acknowledged me at any time, and a black hatred seemed to cloud his face when ever I appeared on the scene. For many years, I hoped we would repair our friendship but he died in a plane crash fulfilling my tongue in cheek prediction for us both. Here was a man that served his country well and faithfully during two tours in Vietnam in Slicks, Cobras, and as an instructor pilot and flew many, many, hours in ag aircraft at night at great risk to himself and family and now he was gone early one Sunday morning under clear blue skies in an experimental airplane an instant after one wing came off in level flight. You never know when the situation will arise when even the best pilot in the world will be out of ideas, altitude and airspeed all at once. His son has become a Naval Aviator and is flying a jet off an aircraft carrier, I know that Buck would be terribly proud.

Chapter Six
Return to Service

For several years partner Bob did not fly. Even when he flew his personal plane, I went along as a safety and morale booster. We were getting more difficult jobs all the time and more and more complaints came in. Finally, one day when one of the staff pilots had a heart attack and another was rolling up a list of violations partner decided he could do as well and dug out his helmet. He began flying again against the wishes of his wife and family. Soon we were the only remaining pilots and we were back in our highly efficient swing. The work was demanding. We fought to take Sundays off. Even then, the bug men would schedule work for the weekend in spite of our protests. If we were really busy it was nothing to fly 10 to twelve hours with earplugs in your ears, and a 7-pound helmet on your head, and lap belts and shoulder harnesses pulled tight. The vibration and noise was gigantic in proportion. After a session of flying all night my ears would ring for hours after even though I wore ear plugs and a well insulated helmet. Within a half an hour the heat flowed from the firewall back to the pilot compartment with the result that the sides of the airplane were very hot to the touch. We did not get out to go to the restroom for fear we would fall behind in our work and slow each other down.

The crews would hand us a burrito and a soda while we were loading and we would eat it on the way to the field holding the stick between our knees. It is funny to contemplate the many hours I have spent with the stick between my knees while eating and as I recall there is no column in my logbook for flight while consuming burritos day or night. In the sixteen years before we got air-conditioning when we finished a nights flying, there would be salt marks in an x across our chest where the shoulder harness and seat belts had been from the constant perspiration from the heat. At night, the temperature would drop to 85 degrees on the ground but once a hundred feet in the air the temperature went back to over a 100 degrees. You could easily tell what time of year it was by looking at the buckle marks on our belts. In winter the belt let out because we weren't working as much and eating a bunch. In summer we sweated a truckload and worked our brains out and didn't feel like eating because of the poison, so we lost weight and the belt would gradually be pulled back in again. During the day, I dreaded doing maintenance because the sun heated everything to a painful level. You had to carry tools in your pockets or keep them in the shade covered with a towel otherwise, you would get a painful burn when you picked them up. We never had a hangar to work in, only a tool shed made from an old rental truck. If it was done, it was done outdoors. Our lives fell into a familiar routine of working six days a week sometimes seven and the years passed. We gained a lot of proficiency and neither one of us had had an accident for a long time.

We now had a flow computer that could be calibrated to a hundredth of a gallon and the little unit had more information than a person could use. The mania against pesticide by the public and fanned by the media caused us to loose some of our most effective pesticides. The price increased nearly ten times for a gallon of pesticide. The laws became more and more restrictive. There was now an 800 number we called a "squeal" line that the public could call to get you in a lot of trouble for a minor infraction. We had to be more and more careful and the pressure to perform with out error was relentless. We tried to get bigger and faster airplanes to cover more acres in less time all the while our price per acre remained nearly the same over the 24 years I sprayed for a living. Prices of parts, insurance, equipment, fuel, and wages all went up except our pay which remained constant, only influenced by how many acres we were able to spray. The years were going by and though I didn't feel any older I was tiring more easily and getting up in the middle of the night to fly in pitch black skies was becoming less attractive. The first night flights of the season increased stress to the max until you got a few hours and began to relax a little. A little was all you dared. We have had fires, generator failures, light failures, broken oil lines, blown cylinder heads, and too many bird strikes. Bird strikes wouldn't seem to be a big problem but they are capable of going through the windshield and making huge dents in the leading edges of the wings. Sometimes they would end up in the oil cooler vent and an immediate landing was necessary before the engine heated up. At night I have seen birds and large bugs go right through the propeller without being touched by the whirling blades, I have witnessed the miracle several times. The hardest time to fly was about three-thirty in the morning. Sleep would come and fatigue was like a giant anchor dragging you down. We soon decided that we would all go to sleep for a half an hour or forty-five minutes and then crank up again. Sometimes we would look up at the black moonless night and see satellites and space junk orbiting overhead. Other nights missile launches from the coast could be seen right up to when they were destroyed and a brilliant fireworks display was the result. We operated near a gunnery range and some nights a transport would drop flares in parachutes which would hang like bright stars just over the horizon to light combat targets like daylight. The sunrises and sunsets were glorious. And there was always the beautiful green panorama of alfalfa fields, row crops, and bare ground all across the horizon. More complaints were cropping up. An incredible array of nut cases would complain any time they saw an Ag aircraft. One night we sprayed cotton with water, iron, and common sugar. A field worker complained that we had sprayed him and went to the hospital. An angry doctor called to demand that we bring an empty sack of the material being sprayed. We took a C&H sugar sack to the hospital. The medic was angered even more when he thought we were trying to pull a fast one on him. Has anyone died from being sprayed with sugar? Another citizen driving down the freeway with the windows up and the air-conditioning on saw a spray plane and went to the hospital with a poison complaint. The wind was blowing

59

away from the freeway. He was smoking at the time, was the poison nicotine? We slowed these kind of complaints by requesting a blood cholinesterase test for complainers. One lady called and angrily demanded that we clean her new aluminum trailer. She accused us of spraying her trailer. We had not sprayed in the vicinity but the county inspector was obligated to investigate. I went along for the ride with the inspector hoping to smooth things over. When he completed his investigation he told the lady there was no law against sand crane shit. When the birds took off from a drain opposite her trailer they lightened the load, directly on the side of her new trailer. One of our pilots was shot at by an angry homeowner on the edge of a cotton field. He managed to put a hole in one of the control surfaces, but the plane landed safely. Although it is a federal offense, the shooter got probation for the act. During dove season hunters would shoot in the direction of our aircraft on the ground and in flight. We used to joke that in September, during dove season, we sat on a trash can lid while we flew. I have actually had BB's roll off the wings while loading next to a drain, from a careless hunter. It was interesting that the doves were always a long distance from the hunters near water or wheat fields. Can doves talk to each other? We got better at staying away from complaints but every field presented new challenges and problems. If a crew was any where near a spraying site we would not spray. It cost us and the grower money. It was not from the danger of pesticide for the danger was nil. Litigation was a new word learned by everyone and they knew we carried lots of insurance, a lucrative target for any ambulance chaser (lawyer). If the field workers needed a day off they would claim they were sick from the non existent poison. Militant Hispanic organizations would supply funds and lawyers for illegals to sue us for any number of reasons. The vendetta backfired one morning when partner sprayed a field a half mile away. A bus was unloading workers and they spotted the aircraft on it's last pass flying away. This was a good time to sting the insured. The foreman called all the dogs, the fire department, the sheriff, ag inspector, and anyone else that would listen. Unfortunately just before this event, the city service groups had undergone hazmat training. So in the cold of morning all, including the men and women, were required to strip while the fire department hosed them down with cold water to remove the imagined offending material. Months of money and time were wasted defending against this kind of attempted extortion. We used all kinds of tricks to extend the life of the pesticides but few would last more than a couple of weeks, some less than a day. I am talking about no detectable residue on sophisticated test equipment. Yet environmentalists still insisted there was great danger. We are all living longer and eating better than ever where's the danger?. Meryl Streep is a great actress, but she doesn't know anything about apples or pesticide yet she cost the Ag industry millions with a simple uninformed comment. Tons of food comes from foreign countries without the pesticide regulation required in the US with out any sickness or death. Each year precious resources in the form of pesticides is outlawed on the premise of safety. It is the protection for our food. Organic food cannot be grown in great quantity, and there is no credible evidence to support that it is any better than pesticide grown food without residue. Third world countries can produce crops much cheaper than we can because of the lack of over regulation. When farming is no longer profitable what will we eat? Crop dusting makes farming profitable.

Chapter Seven
Bigger, Better, Faster

Before I could fly as a crop duster I had to be checked out by Dandy in a 220 horsepower Stearman. The Stearman was actually a Boeing A75 but we called them Stearmans. It was a fabric covered biplane with weighed about three thousand pounds all up. Ours were powered by a 985 cubic inch Pratt and Whitney 450 horsepower radial engine. We flew over in a Piper Colt and rented the 220 Stearman. I had no problems checking out, it was actually fun to fly, it was painted in trainer colors blue and yellow with red and white stripes on the rudder. I thought holy cow they are going to pay me to do this!! My first mount was a 450 Stearman biplane. It carried 185 gallons of material and took off, landed, stalled, and flew at maybe 95 miles an hour with a load on board. The visibility wasn't very good. There was a clever feature regarding the gas gauge on the bottom of the Stearman's center section. It protruded such that a good bird strike would remove it allowing avgas to stream in the pilots face blinding him and eventually catching fire in the process. FAA approved of course. They were fabric covered and burned like a torch when caught on fire. The cockpit wasn't sealed so the wind blew furiously through every nook and cranny. In the winter with layers of clothes and gloves you sat on your hands and held the control stick with your knees on the way to the field to stay warm. We wore a bubble on our helmets instead of goggles, it collected a lot of grease and spray, and if you forgot to snap it down before takeoff it could cause serious damage to your nose if you looked behind you after take off. The Stearman took off easily and flew pretty well in nearly all attitudes, it's only vice was landing in crosswinds nearing it's control limit just before the tail wheel touched. It just went here it wanted to much like an old horse determined to head for the barn. It was amazing how fast a pilot in command became a spectator. We didn't have radios and so one day I told my crew I would throw out a rag with a rock in it to signal when I was done. Well, I finished, and threw the rock/rag out and no one saw it, so much for the visual communication from a no radio biplane. Next I climbed into a Cessna Ag Wagon. It was an all metal monoplane with wing struts which looked like an after thought by an engineer with no confidence. It was a powered glider which carried 175 gallons and flew at 105 miles an hour. The visibility was better but had several blind spots. It had flaps that made it more maneuverable. Some versions were very doggy (the Ag Truck) and took a lot of flying and lighter loads to maintain control under all conditions. They didn't roll very fast so we soon learned to use the rudder to accelerate the roll rate. The Ag Wagon would start slowly then literally snap around the turn. At that point you quickly centered the controls or you entered a spin. They were very noisy, and the flat six cylinder opposed engine held up very well despite the fact that we ran full bore all the time. Once the power was set we didn't touch the throttle until landing, twenty five square was a way of life. (25" &2500 rpm). I did my first night flying in the Ag Wagon. We used little 450 watt lamps. When the lamps were covered with spray after several loads we would get out and wash them with a wet towel, if we didn't, the lights were less effective than a good flashlight. They were easy to take off and land and maintenance was easy because of the quick access with removable panels. The boss where I worked loved to make modifications which included lighted map boards, visors, and other handy gadgets in the cockpit. Once the gadget was approved by him it was installed in all six of the line aircraft. He drank a lot of coffee and needed relief frequently. Not wanting to leave the aircraft he installed a relief tube complete with funnel. He extolled the virtue of this handy feature to one and all. I am still not sure how he did this in flight with belts and clothes on…One day the aircraft was being washed by the clean crew and the tube extending from the belly of the aircraft was pushed up back into the fuselage for cleaning purposes. The next night went by and the next morning the interior of the aircraft had an awful pesticide

odor. The belly interior was sloshing with urine and pesticide. The smell never went away despite all attempts with soap and ammonia. The Agwagon and Agtruck were reliable money makers. Cessna quit making them years ago and many of them are leaving the country, another valuable farm resource endangered each time one crashes.
One of them flew nonstop from Hawaii to Australia in an epic crossing assisted by a Quantas airline captain on his retirement flight. The Ag Wagon landed out of fuel at night, in the rain, on the runway at Sydney, Australia. The Ag Truck was considerably heavier although it looked the same as the wagon. It had wing tanks instead of a fuselage tank and the hopper was larger. The result was a doggy airplane in the heat. For a while I flew a Piper Pawnee with 150 horsepower. It didn't carry much of a load and being fabric covered, fire was always a threat. We used it primarily for dry work with a spreader attached underneath. It's only virtue was that it was cheap to operate. It felt like riding on a giant rubber ball. Beginning our own business we flew the Grumman Ag Cat. It was an aeronautical bumble bee. 13 feet to the top of the top wing it was an all metal biplane with fabric covering on the tail and on the wing undersides. With the Pratt and Whitney 985 it would pack 275 gallons and full fuel and still get airborne in about a quarter of a mile. Compared to other aircraft of it's size the cockpit was cramped and the visibility limited in several directions. It was an extremely docile tail dragger to takeoff and land. It is not a good night flying aircraft because of the limited visibility in a turn. That didn't stop several operations from using it for that purpose. It's crash survivability is legendary. People have survived crashes because of it's well designed crash cage. (cockpit). People love to watch it fly, nearly every time I flew near a freeway, people would stop and watch and ask the flaggers questions about the airplane and pilot.

We bought a Weatherly 201 for a dry airplane. It was a low wing, all metal monoplane, it's looks inspired the name "Jap Zero". It had no flaps and didn't need them and a 450 horsepower Pratt and Whitney Wasp Junior. It had two wing tanks which had to be switched periodically. If you forgot, you had to switch tanks and pump the hand operated fuel pump for all you were worth until the quiet went away and the thunder returned. The oil lines ran through the cockpit and heated the pilot in the winter which was good, but did the same in the summer when it wasn't needed. It would carry 275 gallons all day and run circles around an Ag Cat. When it came time to upgrade, the Air Tractor was chosen next. It is an all metal low wing monoplane with excellent visibility and a 1340 cubic inch 600 hp Pratt and Whitney engine. It's huge flaps and ailerons that droop with the lowering of the flaps make it very maneuverable and easy to take off and land. It is a good night airplane and the amount of work it will crank out is amazing in the hands of a skilled journeyman. One hundred and fifty acres an hour, at fairly high gallonage rates, and upwards of 4-500 acres low volume. It is easy to maintain and rugged for dirt strip operations. Ours were equipped with air-conditioning and GPS operated flagging systems in latter years. The air-conditioning reduced the fatigue and the GPS freed us from the restraints that human flaggers caused by not showing up. Our work output increased by some thirty percent and reduced operating costs of wages, workman's comp, and insurance. Before GPS, a good chaser was a necessity. I was lucky enough to have one of the best. Duh-Duh was a fierce pickup driver that could set fields as fast as I could fly them. Her fearless herding of the flaggers and driving in impossible conditions day and night kept things humming. My self confidence was bolstered when I knew she was going to flag for me. I could fly herbicide closer, and target material with her I wouldn't try with others. Another called

65

"Oklahoma" was probably a rum runner. On trips back and forth to the load airstrip, I would clear the roads of highway patrol cars and the like so she could get an all clear on the radio, sometimes it looked to me like she was keeping up with me in the airplane. Glad I wasn't riding in that truck!

Chapter Eight
Surviving the Gauntlet

Over the years events would occur that would test my resolve as an Ag pilot. They are commonly called hairy situations. In Fairy Tales they start out "Once upon a time", GI's commonly say " This is no shit", but the end is a story which stretches your imagination. Embellishment is a wonderful thing to use in a story, it allows you to beef up the good parts and leave out the embarrassing ones so that one is viewed in the most favorable light. So it is that I will recount some of the most notable occurrences during my life as an Ag pilot. In my early experience I got most of the small and dangerous fields. One of the fields was named the Widow Patch. It was a field that was situated next to a steep mesa with a diagonal power line across the middle third and power lines across one side and end. The trick was to fly under the middle set and over the end set then climb the mesa a couple of hundred feet then turn low to the ground and then dive into the field from above the other direction. As the cotton grew higher the clearance between the gas tank vent and the power line grew less and less, each time raising my blood pressure by a couple of points. Then on completion of the field, trim passes would be laid on each side of the wires to assure coverage. The ride back after that job was always a welcome event. A person's cholinesterase level decreases with exposure to dangerous chemicals. When working on the airplanes it was easy to get your hands in the stuff because it was all over the airplane and along with other places your level would decrease. If you stayed away for a weekend or so your level would come back up. The dicey part comes when you get some chemical on you and your level is already low. Then the nausea sets in and the sweats occur on the upper lip and forehead. The pupils get small and dizziness occurs. If you are lucky you can get antidote pills, usually atropine tablets. If you aren't, a trip to the emergency room is in order rather quickly. I wasn't sick many times in 25 years, but when it gets you there is no way out, it is better to be careful and avoid contact. One of the points of contact is windshield cleaning. We used a common dust cleaner to clean the windshield but the chemicals would transfer to the cloth and then to your hands. A days flying and several cleanings would expose you to a lot of chemical. People that smoke are familiar with the onset of poisoning as the nicotine in the cigarettes is deadly poison; the early poisoning symptoms are the familiar buzz and lift that smoker's experience. One of the other side effects is what I call the angry personality. As a result of being exposed to pesticides Ag pilots especially when tired, are irritable, angry, have wild mood swings, and can be bellicose. It just comes with the territory. (Although I know many people in other occupations with the same traits). In twenty five years of flying and being exposed to all manner of pesticides and herbicides I only witnessed a single case of poisoning that was life threatening and never saw or heard of a poison fatality. Our flaggers were always up wind and rarely got sprayed if they were positioned properly. Power lines are a concern to all ag pilots and anyone that fly's close to the ground. We checked the fields closely before flying from the ground and later we would make several turns around the field to locate guy wires and other obstructions. After a while you begin to understand how the lines are hooked up and look for them where others wouldn't see them. Most airplanes will go through a 12,000 volt three phase line by just adding power and putting the spinner or prop hub on the line. The result will probably be some prop burns or possibly some marks on the leading edges. Phone lines are also easy to transit through. The large lines that run down the main thorough fares and high tension lines which have half inch stainless cores and small cables which are difficult to see from tower to tower are another matter altogether, better to give them a large leeway and stay clear. There is no getting through them, under or over but not through. Going under power lines is not a big deal if you understand some fundamentals. One of the first is never fly under wires you are not familiar with towards clutter. By clutter, I mean houses, mountains or other obstacles that might mask a wire from view. You should be able to see sky below the wires and therefore see other guy wires, phone lines or signs and pumps sticking up in the flight path. If you can't see, fly a pass the other direction against clear sky and be sure it is clear before flying under the other direction. Secondly, I liked to trim the aircraft a little nose up so that you hold pressure forward a little while flying in the ground effect bubble. Holding pressure forward so that you get the aircraft as close as possible to the ground or the crop without hitting it you wait for the feel and the sound. When you hear cotton boles slapping the tires you are too low. Flying in ground effect is a learned art, most pilots only experience it for a short time during takeoff and landing. After a while an ag pilot can feel it and use it to his advantage while operating heavily loaded aircraft. On clearing the wires above or below wait till you are clear before initiating a turn. I have had three wire strikes in twenty five years and one is too many. Aircraft problems are few but when they occur you have to deal with them the best you can. One night while flying a Grumman Ag Cat my alternator went out and soon the lights went from white to red and finally dim. I shut off all power and flew around in circles in the dark until a solution occurred, my partner showed up and I dropped in behind him and used his lights to land. While ferrying a Thrush I flew till dark and discovered that the lights had failed en route. I did the circling trick till a light twin landed and I followed him in using his lights, I don't think he knew I was there at all. We use a device called a smoker. It is a pump with a line to the exhaust. It pumps oil into the flame in the exhaust and causes smoke to belch out. It is used to see if the drift is towards people or a susceptible crop. One day on the way to the field the chaser said "Hey Ron do you have your smoker on?", the smoke I was trailing was from a sick engine not from the smoker, and I beat a hasty retreat back to the airfield. I always thought the carburetor would hold enough fuel so that if the engine pump quit only an occasional pump of the aux pump would keep me flying. One afternoon I was spraying and the engine quit abruptly. I immediately pumped the emergency fuel boost pump for all I was worth and the engine started again. Trouble is when I quit pumping so did the engine, the airplane bobbed and weaved as I flew with one hand and pumped with the other....all the way home. When I finally lined up with the runway I stopped pumping and coasted on to the airstrip. I only had one engine failure at night in several thousand hours of night crop spraying. Heading towards the field I could see the flaggers flashlights and a quick look at the instruments showed all in the green but something was wrong. I could hear it even though I wore ear plugs and an expensive helmet. The airplane was slowing with its heavy load and I called on the radio and let everyone know that I had a problem. I dumped the load over an empty field and made it back to a dirt strip nearby. After landing I could hear the number two cylinder puffing with its cylinder head loose and hanging by the rubber hoses. I only had eight of the nine cylinders working. It was a fairly common occurrence and I have put out the remainder of a load with only eight cylinders working, but only in daylight. I once had a Cessna Ag Wagon develop a crack in the crankshaft spewing oil all over the windshield. Soon I couldn't see ahead so I opened the side door with a loud bang and looked out the side. After landing my face looked like I worked at an oil well. Sometimes there are problems you didn't know were hiding in the airplane all along and one day they come along to scare the wits out of you. I was flying an airplane that had a spray handle that was bent at a strange angle when we bought it. You turned on the spray with the handle which was attached to the spray valve under the belly of the aircraft. It's operation never caused a problem because when spraying the throttle was full forward. One day while loading the plane with chemical, I was by myself with the load hose hooked to the airplane. The flaggers were waiting and all set up. I was having difficulty moving the spray valve because of friction in the

70

valve caused by some of the gritty powders used in the chemical. I thought while I was waiting I would loosen it up with a pair of vise grip pliers. I crawled under the airplane and with the pliers I began to push and pull furiously to loosen up the errant valve. All of a sudden it let loose and the handle swung forward to the throttle with a healthy wallop and slammed the throttle forward to it's full throttle position. I can tell you that fear accelerates you to miraculous speeds, the same I used to get out from under and on top of the wing to pull back the throttle. If it were not for the load hose hooked to the airplane I wouldn't have had the precious seconds needed to get from under to over and save the airplane from damage. I carefully checked all airplanes I flew for unseen gotcha's but some you don't notice until a special set of conditions exists. Some chemicals and their application are very dangerous even when precautions are followed to the letter. Dusting Sulfur is one of those. It is usually applied in no wind or low drift conditions. Early one morning I was dusting melons with sulfur. We would leave the engine run with the airplane pointed into the wind usually that would keep the powder out of the exhaust and off the red hot engine manifolds. As the load truck bucket moved over the opened hopper door, my loader tripped the handle to allow the dust to fall through a sock like guide to the hopper. We had wet the ground around the airplane, the truck had static chains, and the airplane was bonded. The sulfur dust was boiling out of the leaks and cracks of the bucket when suddenly, like a gasoline explosion, the dust burst into flame. The pillar of fire was enormous and I could feel the intense heat through the plastic windshield. My loader took off like a shot and hit the ground running. I thought I could blow out the flames by advancing the throttle but the fire was using all the oxygen and though I opened the throttle all the way nothing happened, the engine would barely idle. By now I had been holding my breath for some time, trying not to breathe the fumes of the burning sulfur. I could see the flames licking out below the wing at the trailing edge all around the gas tanks.

I knew it wouldn't be long before it blew. The loader in the truck recovered from the shock of seeing the fire and began to back the now burning bucket away from the airplane, which was still burning. I wasn't wearing a respirator (mistake 1) and I wasn't wearing leather gloves to protect my hands. (mistake 2) It seemed like an eternity before I finally leaped out of the burning airplane. Except for passing out momentarily in the airplane, I wasn't seriously hurt. I was one of the lucky ones....several Ag pilots have died or been seriously injured in sulfur fires both in the air and on the ground. Why is it used? It works to make the soil more acidic and chases the spiders and mites away, and it is cheap for the grower. The risk to the pilot and airplane is never considered. Some operators won't put the stuff on at any price. One day I only had a couple of loads to do, so I mixed the chemicals and put a load in, and took off for a distant field. On the way I saw smoke curling up from a not too distant point. When the conditions were right, the stubble in fields was burned to keep host plants from providing shelter for wintering bugs. As I passed over the smoke I looked down and was surprised to see the tail section of an Ag Cat! The crash must have just happened before I got there. I circled again and saw that *two* Ag Cats were in pieces in the field below me. After finishing a field, Brand x Cropdusters were trimming the field one aircraft on each side of the field as they passed under the wires at the end of the field they both pulled up and turned towards each other, each hidden by the biplanes top wing. On impact one Cat impaled the other mid fuselage killing Dandy my check pilot instantly. The other pilot was injured but survived the mid air collision, and as far as I know is still flying. Another job I took for a short time involved the largest airplane I ever flew. A fellow ag pilot was flying tankers in off periods. Enormous fires started in Southern California and all tankers were needed that could fly. I was asked if I wanted to copilot a Douglas DC7. All I had to do was three takeoffs and landings and I was hired. Well almost. At the base where the tanker was, someone was shooting touch and goes with a no radio Luscombe. As I made each circuit, the Luscombe turned base and final just ahead of me so I had to go around. Gear up, gear down, power settings, there is a lot to do even with help from the pilot. It took a while but we were finally on our way to a military base where we would be staged. On landing we were not allowed to park on the ramp because the big 3350's dripped oil like a busted refinery. During operations, the hydraulic system started leaking fluid called Skydrol. We had to open the windows and make an emergency landing breathing like dogs leaning out of a pickup. Down in the access hell hole we discovered a cracked block which connected the hydraulics, we soon were covered in the stuff and discovered another problem. Skydrol burns your skin. We were going to look for parts but first a stop at a motel to shower. The shower seemed to make the burning worse. Finally got the problem fixed, then a brake went out. The brake disks had broken and were jammed up in the wheel. So on the taxiway we had to jack up the wheel. The first attempt resulted in driving the jack through the pavement. Wood planks evened the load and we finally pried the broken parts out and got the brakeless wheel back on. By this time I was thinking being a tanker pilot was not all it was cracked up to be. On the flight home I added up my expenses and pay and they were nearly even. When we set up for landing we noticed that hydraulic pressure was falling at an alarming rate. On final, Beetle announced that we probably wouldn't have brakes and maybe no nose wheel steering. He did a fantastic job and we barely made the 180 down the runway to taxi back for parking. When we shut down, I opened the door and threw the knotted rope down to the ground and climbed down from the cockpit. On the way down Skydrol was dripping from the belly like a thin waterfall. That was the last of my tanker career. I ferried several ag airplanes across the US. One in particular, was a fifty-eight foot span monster that grossed six tons or more. It sported a huge 4 blade prop and a large Russian radial engine. It packed 600 gallons of spray and

188 gallons of fuel. It gulped about 65 gallons of fuel an hour. Just climbing up the side to get in was a project. The boss asked me if I wanted to go get the new airplane, and since things were slow I thought it would be a great idea. He flew me to Las Vegas in his plane and I got a flight to Raleigh-Durham, North Carolina. It's an all day ordeal and this was before 9-11-01. I arrived there at night and although I had faxed my arrival there was no one there to pick me up. So I rented a car and headed for Smithfield where the aircraft was located. I stumbled around in the dark for a while and finally located a motel and crashed. The next morning I headed for the airstrip. There were no apologies for hanging me out to dry the night before so I assumed that's the way they did business. These aircraft are shipped in pieces and assembled here and modified for use in the US. The airplane I was to fly was nearing completion and test flight. There was a modification done on the elevator to add servo trim tabs to make the controls easier to use. It was installed by the fellow that had the STC for the modification, and therefore FAA approved. I had to return the car and I was to pick up a contract ferry pilot from Raleigh-Durham and when I asked what he looked like the secretary told me he looks like Santa Claus. Sure enough, when I pulled up to the load zone, out the door came a fellow that looked like Santa. I was going to spend some time as a tourist on the east coast but the weather was clearing and the Santa was heading west and he kindly offered to let me tag along for the first thousand miles. It is a good thing he did. My hands were full of nasty airplane, and navigation was not high on my list of things to do. After the test flight no mention was made of the strange flight characteristics of the aircraft so I assumed it was ok and loaded my stuff in and I took off behind the other pilot. His comment to me was, " you've got it up cowboy, now lessee if you can git it down". As soon as I was airborne the airplane was unstable in pitch. What that means is when you pull back the nose pitches up, and the pressure on the control stick gets greater and greater until you have to push the other direction to stop it. The same is

74

true of the other direction. When you pushed down it kept moving down till you pulled back and stopped it. I had taken my video camera and 35 mm camera to document the flight, but the airplane was a hand full and it was all I could do initially just to stay in loose formation with my new friend leading me west, so I took very few pictures. My first landing was uneventful even though it looked like I was several stories above the ground. We taxied in and refueled, checked for oil leaks, and began to taxi out. During our refuel, several bus loads of school kids unloaded along the fence. Not sure if it was a field trip or just a casual stop, but they were watching intently through the fence. Santa keyed the mike and asked," do you think you can make a formation takeoff?". I replied in the affirmative and we slowly pulled out on the wide runway and began adding power. We thundered off into the blue and left the wide eyed kids in a cloud of smoke. It isn't every day you get to see that kind of aircraft take off or land. Santa was going south to a convention display, so we said our goodbyes and I continued west to Crosset, Arkansas for a propeller change. I flew all day till sundown and had a hard time finding the airport in the setting sun. As I crossed a row of trees there was the strip. After landing the folks help me tie the critter down and took me to a motel for a much needed rest. With a new prop, I was airborne west. Landing in Texas, I found a ride into town and asked for a ride in early in the morning. I was told the best hamburger in the world was next door at a truck stop. Sure enough a large hamburger was delivered on a large platter with a mound of fries falling off the plate. It was in fact the best I ever had. I was picked up in the dark of morning to find fog everywhere. I waited and waited and called weather. While waiting I didn't know there was going to be an air show to celebrate the re-opening of the newly refurbished airport. Sky divers appeared along with all sorts of aircraft. Through the fog a Stinson L5 appeared and landed. I asked him where he came from and he replied that he had just left Childress west of there and it was clear a few miles west. With a ring of CAP cadets around me I

75

taxied out and took off as the unintended opening of the air show. West to Childress, I was getting used to the monster but still not comfortable I continued west through Texas, New Mexico, and Arizona. On the leg from Childress to Tucumcari I burned 168 gallons of the available 188 on board, my groundspeed was near 85 miles per hour....I was told at the factory the fuel consumption would increase with altitude but they didn't know by how much. I found out it was a lot... When I got home, we flew the beast several weeks before we discovered the pushrods installed in the modification were too short causing the strange malady in the flight characteristics. It was still a handful, and my boss later crashed on takeoff, he was not injured, but the aircraft was totaled. I didn't miss flying it one bit. The boss bought another one and had Santa deliver it. I was glad it wasn't me.

Chapter Nine
My Other Job

Over the years my electronic training has been very useful at times. For a while I was involved in design and liaison engineering for all sorts of solid state and digital electronic equipment and devices. Everything from biomedical to nuclear and even did a stint in electronic calibration. After I had been out of the electronic business for several years I received a phone call from the local radio station. They wanted to know if I could look at their transmitter. I tried to explain that my training in the military was for mostly vacuum tubes and I was interrupted by a whoop and a yell "that's great that's what we have!" I went down to work on the aging transmitter. I didn't know it then, but on that day I became Chief Engineer of an AM-FM broadcast station and remained so for twenty years...

The transmitter showed years of neglect and abuse. Burn marks, loose wires, and bypassed safety switches were everywhere. I managed to get it running but I cautioned that it wouldn't last long, it had seen better days. The manager with visions of expanding horizons had ordered a state of the art, computer controlled, transmitter. Without consulting me or the owner he had ordered the most complex high powered unit that money could buy. When it arrived I was shocked to find that it was mounted on a large flatbed semi-trailer truck. The two units weighed several thousand pounds together. The small winding road to the transmitter site would not accommodate the big semi so I soon commandeered a fork lift and a smaller truck to move the new equipment to its new home. I cut the back of the building out and slid the old transmitter out and pushed the new one in with drill pipe and the fork lift. After the wall was reinstalled it took a while for me to figure out how to wire this new beast up for operation. Soon the desert was rocking to the new sound of a brand new transmitter. In the middle of this I was still flying crop dusting airplanes day and night as well as doing maintenance on the aircraft.

Some days I would just stare at the maze of books and schematics with a snoot full of poison and wish it would all go away. I soon grew adept at troubleshooting and repairing the transmitter and all the studio equipment. It seemed like the only time it broke down was when I was flying my brains out and the desert was at its hottest. The station was a welcome diversion from the stress of constant day in day out flight operations. It ended up being a state-of-the-art station completely automated including the capability to command the station from a remote telephone location. The owner was supportive and soon the station was making money from a previously unprofitable situation. I was so tired from flying long hours at night that sometimes I would just sit in the transmitter building and wait for an inspiration, I had no clue what was wrong or how to fix it. My sub-conscious was my salvation. Several days after confronting the problem or problems the solution would dawn on me and away I would go to the next step. Working on transmitters with that kind of voltage and current is very dangerous and so each step is carefully considered before proceeding, to negate the probability that I could instantly become a crispy critter. I usually worked on it when no one was around so if I was injured there would be no help. Thousands of volts and many amps could terminate my flying career in an instant. Flying at night, the value of my subconscious would be evident in the ability to "see" things after I passed them moving at nearly 200 feet per second. As I flew over an obstruction I would see it in detail minutes later and even remember writing on signs nailed to power poles. At times I had dreams of flying at incredible speeds close to the ground, and every minute detail was in focus and color. Perception in my life had become reality. Flying at night was like being in a large bowl of small lights whirling and darting in every conceivable direction, somehow my mind would unscramble the input and keep me oriented so that I made the turns and ended up precisely on the swath run regardless of the airplane and it's environment. I am not sure how all this happens, I don't think you can train someone to do it. Not unlike the honey bee we could fly to a field at night without flaggers and trim before they got there and set up the field. Some times we would trim several fields while waiting for crews. After a thunderstorm it was sometimes too wet to allow a flag pickup to get to the field to flag it, so we used a technique where we would divide the swaths into telephone pole spans, culvert spaces, and rows in adjacent fields. We would spray the entire field with out flaggers by just eyeballing the swaths. I Never had a complaint using this procedure. I did get some complaints using flaggers occasionally. The sights and sounds of night flying are very different from day.. For me they are completely different with night flying being the most tiring. A lot of the visual cues used in day are absent and you have to substitute other procedures for safe flight. High rates of closure are avoided, shallower descents. It takes more time to crop dust at night for safety sake so the work output is necessarily less than day. In summary crop dusting at night is like an intense video game where you get to live one more day if you win.

Chapter Ten
Tools of the Trade

Vision is your most important asset in crop dusting. Besides flying the aircraft, you must be able to identify various crops and locations. To spot obstacles and wires and you must do all of this day and night. I am not an eye doctor but here are a couple of items to think about. Your eyes consume about 25 percent of the total nervous energy of your body. If you read a lot or do a lot of instrument flying expect to be tired. The same goes for night Ag flying. Wear dark shades during the day (I am told that the sun bleaches out the purple fluid in your eyes reducing your night vision.) Wear clear at night if you use prescription glasses. Do not use the auto dark lenses in daytime they aren't dark enough and they aren't clear enough at night. You can try to wear contacts but my experience with them has been that the chemicals cause burning sensation in the eyes that is very unpleasant not to mention the dust and dirt found on dirt strips in outlying areas, which also conspire to limit vision. There are many new laser oriented and surgical procedures that promise better vision for flyers coming into use every day. Fly early morning and evening swaths near dangerous obstacles and wires down sun. (with the sun at your back). Looking directly into the sun, flaggers, wires, and other obstructions are invisible. If you must do it, use a dark visor on the helmet along with sunglasses. Don't do anything dumb like using a grinder, wire wheel, or other device that would shoot a particle into your unguarded eye. Your career as an Ag pilot could be over along with several other jobs the instant you loose your sight. Protecting your hearing is high on the list, maybe not today but in the future if you want to be able to hear your favorite music, peoples conversation, and movie dialog with out the accompaniment of ringing in your ears it is best that you use earplugs. Some work, some don't. They are all un-sanitary and after many hours painful to wear, but an absolute necessity. Over the years I have used a squeeze bulb to irrigate my ears to clear wax and dirt accumulated from using earplugs. The same goes for the nose and sinuses; I used baking soda and salt to clear dirt. A good quality helmet is helpful for good communications as it houses your boom mike and headset. It also reduces noise to some extent if properly constructed and fitted. In my many years of flying I have worn out several crash helmets, they were all expensive. I always wore 100% cotton clothing while crop dusting. Not just because I supported the cotton industry, but also because in the event of fire it wouldn't stick to your skin the way polyester would. I always carried a good quality flashlight or lacking that two cheap ones at night. In the cockpit I had a notebook, a pair of vise grips, and a combination screwdriver. We used a popular lemon scented furniture polish to clean the windshield. Over the years, we must have used a truckload of the stuff and never damaged a windshield. Sometimes the buildup of pesticide gets so great that only avgas will take the residue off and then the polish is used to take the gas residue off. A good pocketknife is necessary for cutting sacks of seed; a 4" crescent wrench is always helpful for adjustments to the spreader or boom brackets. Carry a pair of lightweight leather gloves for protection from fire. A high quality carefully fitted respirator is a necessity. My respirator fits on brackets mounted on the sides of the helmet. Use the chinstrap on every flight; snug your shoulder harness before takeoff. If you don't your helmet will go through the windshield in a crash and your shoulders will be broken if your harness isn't snug. I originally wore boots all the time and still think it is a good idea to protect your legs from the residue inherent in most wash racks. If you are going to apply flammable material (read sulfur), a Nomex flight suit isn't a bad idea and a necessity for government contracts. Ditto Nomex gloves. I tried to buy pants that were too long and cut off the legs to make extra pockets below the knee so that glasses and other items used in flight were accessible with the shoulder harness in place. I kept records of chemicals applied and

81

hours flown for the log book entries. We were required to get 20 units of continuing education each two years just to maintain our Ag pilot license. We took a biannual flight review to keep our commercial pilots license along with a second class medical. I had to take a check ride every two years to maintain my flight instructor rating and renew my inspection authorization yearly in March, so you can see I spent a lot of time working for the government for free. The continuing education usually had little to do with the job and was conjured up by Phd's that had little or no practical knowledge of the trade or discipline.

Chapter Eleven
Dealing with Big Brother

It is interesting to study what happens to our fellow man when he is given power. It doesn't seem to matter what level of government, incompetence is the rule. It isn't about safety, it's about control. There is no extreme to far to be considered as a requirement by a bureaucrat. We sheep people allow nearly any extreme as long as it doesn't affect us directly. Time is very important when dealing with insect raids on food supply. Overnight is too long in most instances. Yet we are required to submit a notice of intent 24 hours in advance of spraying a field. Now mind you no one is notified of the coming event. Not the old woman in the house bordering the field to be sprayed. She may have asthma or some respiratory condition. She has moved from the big city pollution to the country where there is more pollen, pesticide, herbicide, farm smoke, cattle dust, than you can imagine and searches for clean air. The crews that work in the field and individuals jogging on the ditch banks are clueless. Almost no one knows of the impending application. Anyone could call and inquire but no one does. Of course you would have to call every day to find out and you would soon tire of that. So the crop duster shows up in the dark of early morning and begins an application in an environment designed to criminalize him or her. There is actually an 800 number to report a leaky nozzle or any irregularity noticed while the hapless pilot is plying his trade. Most county employees don't know a swirl plate from an egg roll yet they are empowered with the same authority as a police officer. They can ground your airplane and set you up for fines and imprisonment. Once the accusation is made it is very difficult to prove your innocence in our guilty till proven innocent society. At one time there existed a cooperation between applicator and powers that be such that you could comfortably tell on yourself and everyone worked to improve the situation. There were small fines but the atmosphere was one of working to get the job done. It is different now, you are basically guilty until proven innocent, any person can make an accusation and you are in for months of agony and paper work. Our government is criminalizing our daily actions to the point that our towns are becoming like small third world countries where you are smart to keep quiet, deny everything, and give only name, rank, and serial number. If this sounds paranoid you are dead right they are out to get you, well not exactly you, they just want to separate you from your license to earn a living and the money you earned doing it. They were all nice people before joining the FAA, or the State, or County, but once empowered with the title and position they get the God Complex and so are passing judgment and sentence, and execution with all the concern of purchasing an ice cream cone. My hat is off to the few. Those that would help you wend your way through the endless red tape. They would go the extra mile to help when they see you going the wrong way. Occasionally they would look the other way when you exhibit poor judgment or and occasional lack of discipline. They would not criminalize you for an occasional error when you were really trying to do a good job. But unfortunately they are the very, very, few and dwindling. The FAA has the power to take your license, fine you and imprison you without any trial, without a jury, and without due process. Administrative errors in filling out paper work and log books can cost the hapless owner and mechanic thousands of dollars in fines and suspension of license which would cause a loss of employment. The FAA can interpret the regulations in any one of several ways to suit their case or cause. The current head of the FAA is not a pilot, has no aviation experience, and is in a position to set policy and procedure for our nations aviation community. The procedures for paperwork through the FAA are becoming more and more complex and often employees of the FAA have no experience or knowledge of the field or subject they may rule or control. They may use other branches of the FAA to reject applications for safety modifications to limit the litigation and liability for any change they may approve. The longer I work in this industry the more I wonder why anyone would want to work this hard and expose themselves to the danger and loss of income, not to mention the possibility of prison. Risking your life for a head of lettuce or a bale of cotton is one thing, but the random heavy handed enforcement of minor infractions makes no sense. It is all done in the guise of safety and protecting the environment all the while looking the other way for large corporate or government abuses. You are right, I chose to do this job, mostly for the love of flying and I looked a long time for a job that suited me and was involved in aviation. I tried flight instructing, corporate flying, fire bombing, helicopter and fixed wing ag work, I have towed gliders and dropped skydivers, and I had a choice to do or not do any of them. So I guess you could say I deserved what I got. I am a living dinosaur, a few years from now I think people won't know that crop dusters ever existed. As a group we provided a lot of food and fiber for a lot of people and a lot of us died to do it, I was just lucky enough to avoid the rush to eternity

Chapter Twelve
In The Long Run

The many years of precision flying in all kinds of weather, day and night has had some interesting repercussions in my life. I can still pass a second class medical exam with no restrictions and I use no medications. My hearing is of course diminished by the constant din of large radial engines and helicopter transmissions. I have worn an expensive helmet all my Ag flying life along with earplugs but I still have tinnitus, a ringing in my ears that never goes away. One of my loaders asked me why I wore such an expensive helmet and offered that he could buy one for 85 dollars (mine cost upwards of 900 dollars). I replied that if you have an 85 dollar head you wear an 85 dollar helmet, mine I feel is worth considerably more than that. My reflexes are amazingly quick for my age and of course my experience helps to keep me out of trouble that requires quick responses and great piloting ability. With over 16,000 thousand hours in Ag work I can't say yet if the constant exposure to pesticides and herbicides and various aircraft chemicals and fluids has cost me. The jury is still out on that subject. Ag pilots are getting older before they retire if they get past the testosterone stage. Pilots don't last long that have the cowboy attitude in an airplane. In the past years I have survived many close scrapes, engine failures, chemical exposure, nausea, exhaustion from heat and other sources. I have done a lot of flying, learning as I went. Survival is what I learned best. You have to decide when to take the risk, and when you are going to pass. Thunderstorms at night were a formidable obstacle. They arrived suddenly and sometimes I had to make a run for it to land in safety, tie the airplane down, only to be pelted by flying rocks and rain minutes after. I was after all, very lucky. I made mistakes along the way. Although I did most of the maintenance on my work and personal aircraft I never had a failure or aircraft malfunction caused by my work. Sure I had cylinders blow, valves fail, alternators that burned up, lights that burned out, and propellers that failed to cycle, but I usually made it back to base and fixed them to fly later in the day or night. I didn't think I would live very long so I didn't prepare myself financially for retirement. So while my contemporaries are receiving checks monthly from their employers from their retirement, I ended up with no retirement income. I always worked for a commission and none of my employers was concerned about medical insurance and retirement until the last months of my employment. Soon after I left my last job my health insurance ran out and I immediately contracted a particularly virulent form of pneumonia losing a great deal of my savings in the process. So I again lucked out and recovered from a potentially fatal illness. If I still owned an Ag operation I would still be flying. I still enjoy hanging out at the airport, I love sailing, and of course working with my hands. Early in the morning when the air is cool and the skies are clear I loved to roll my trusty Citabria out of it's hangar strap myself in and go flying. I had to sell it because my lack of income couldn't pay for tie down and insurance now incredibly expensive and increasing because of the mania for security at airports. Insurance for flying for those over 60 is more dear all the time and nearly unavailable for anything with high performance. As a result a lot of people fly "barefoot" with no insurance. All these wonderful flying hours and years, suspended as a bird in the sky I have watched all those that struggle on the ground to make a living. They may be rich or famous or many other things but they have never experienced the flow of adrenalin on a takeoff in a heavily overloaded Ag airplane. Tensely waiting for any sign that the tail may lift and when it does watching for signs that the aircraft will come to life and carry me to the field. On my way I sail over canals, multi-hued fields, homes and farmers operating their equipment, each making a crop to clothe or feed millions, and I in my machine a small but necessary part of the whole picture. I have made the world swirl and turn and spin at my feather touch on the controls, an incredible dance macabre with the insect world. On every pass I try to make the next better than the last, faster, closer, cleaner, more efficient. I am becoming a computer that watches, controls, observes, changes, and responds to the metal avian body I call my aircraft. With all my experience, with all my desire to use an airplane for something useful, with all my passing days I was first, foremost, and lastly a bug killer. Clarence "Kelly " Johnson the famous aircraft designer of the famed SR 71 Blackbird in his book "More Than My Share Of It All" makes the statement, "Not all of our weapons are military. Some are economic. The most important airplane for the future, to my way of thinking, isn't a transport, isn't a bomber, isn't a fighter. It is the crop duster. Why? We are going to have to feed an awful lot of people in this world. We must keep our ecology in hand, save our forests, seed the fields, fight the fires, control weather, and even - should there be nuclear explosions and environmental contamination- spray to accelerate the diminution of radiation. There is nothing dramatic about this airplane. It just might be the airplane most important to more people than any other. I'd like to think that airplane was one for peaceful purposes." Kelly Johnson never designed an ag aircraft......

Chapter Thirteen
What's It Really Like

Someone asked me "What is it like to fly crop dusting day and night?" My first answer trying to be funny, is put a seven pound helmet on your head, bind your shoulders and waist with straps, set a big CD boom box in front of the dryer and turn it up full volume near the threshold of pain, spray some Raid in the dryer and climb in after setting the timer to ten hours on the dryer. Have someone let you out after five hours and turn the lights out and climb back in for another five hours. If you really want to be authentic have someone bring you a hamburger or burrito and a soda you can eat with one hand when the lights go out. Well that's kind of stretching it, here's the way it really is. A grower or farmer usually hires an entymologist to monitor his fields for damage by various pests. When the "bug man" as he is called finds damage he identifies the pest and decides which pesticide treatment is needed and writes a NOI (notice of intent to spray) which is filed with the county usually 24 hours before the field is to be sprayed. This goes to the Pesticide vendor. They fill the order with the necessary adjuvants and pesticide. It is then delivered to the aerial applicator. (crop duster) Actually crop duster is a misnomer because most of aerial application is done by spraying (pesticide diluted with water). The office help at the crop dusting operation checks the order for accuracy and counts the material. The field is mapped with cross streets or irrigation gate numbers or hand drawn maps. When the pilot comes in he checks the work order, the map, and the calculations for the loads to cover the field. In this business the man (or woman) that pulls the handle is responsible for the application, if something goes wrong, he gets hung. Not the bug man, not the office help, or even the owner. So it is necessary to be sure everything is correct before making the application. Depending on the load capacity of the aircraft and the difficulty of the field location the aircraft is loaded light or heavy depending on the situation. For example if the order calls for 5 gallons per acre and there are 70 acres then 350 gallons are required. A 400 gallon machine will easily accommodate this load size. A 300 gallon machine will require two 175 gallon loads to complete the job. The pilot takes his maps and work orders to the airplane with his helmet and ear plugs and loads them aboard. He checks the oil and fuel and looks at the engine and airframe. If there are nozzle shutoffs for the purpose of raising or lowering the spray rate on the spray booms then they have to be set before flight to the high or low position. With the aircraft still tied down, a cockpit check is made to make sure the throttle is closed and the mixture and magnetos are "off". The prop is pulled through nine times to make sure there is no hydraulic lock in the bottom cylinders of the radial engine to prevent damage on startup. He now unties the aircraft and climbs in and begins startup procedure. All electrical and radios are turned off and a check is made to be sure the spray fan brake is on so that the pump won't run dry and ruin the pump seal on the way to the load truck. When the master is turned on the voltage is checked to be sure the work/wire/turn lights are off. Everyone has their own procedure for starting a radial engine. We used the wobble pump to bring the fuel pressure up then primer to prime nine times and then closed it. Then stroke the throttle twice or as many times as necessary to feel a resistance to movement caused by the presence of fuel and crack (move it a half inch forward) it for starting. After a visual check and yell "clear" the engine is cranked and when it lights it is set at idle and the oil pressure is checked for an increase. Some smoke is usually present and some oil spots if the aircraft has been sitting for a while is normal. The oil pressure is checked for a positive increase and while the engine is warming up the helmet comm lines are connected and the maps/orders are mounted to a clip board in the cockpit. The GPS computer is set for swath width and chemical rate and type of spray procedure, I.e. ends to the middle, round robin, or back and forth. As the aircraft moves out of it's parking place the brakes are tested immediately. If at night, the lights are tested on the roll to the load truck. What the pilot is looking for io any ieason to abort the flight *before* the load is put in the hopper. Once the load is in, if an abort occurs, the load has to be pumped out to a holding tank for another aircraft. To taxi the aircraft in a turn the pilot has to push the stick forward to unlock the tail wheel which locks straight ahead when the stick is pulled aft. On the roll to the load truck the pilot calls the chaser to determine if the field is clear of people, animals, or any reason why the application should not be made. The chaser is in a vehicle adjacent the field and he/she gives the wind direction and velocity, and any other needed info such as susceptible crops, live stock, standing water, presence of bee's, or work crews adjacent the target field. On arrival at the load truck the loader attaches the hose to the airplane and waits for the signal from the pilot to start the load into the hopper. The pilot can see the liquid in the fiberglass hopper and when the level nears the needed mark hand signals are used to signal cut-off. The hose is removed and the aircraft begins to taxi to the active runway or in some cases begins the takeoff roll as soon as the loader is in the truck with the windows rolled up to protect from blowing dirt and rocks. As the takeoff roll progresses a power check is made to make sure the engine is developing full power and all operating gauges are in the green arcs. Some aircraft will allow you to push forward on the stick to get the tail up and pick up speed faster, others will come up on their own time just by holding the stick neutral. At some point a judgment has to be made on whether or not the aircraft will become airborne in the allotted distance. It is prudent to keep one hand on the dump handle to allow the dumping of a small portion of the load in case of emergency. It is rarely needed but better to be safe than sorry. Once airborne the flaps are retracted (if so equipped) and the engine is set to working numbers for manifold pressure and propeller rpm. Heading to the field in earlier times we looked for the flagger on the corner of the field. The pilot lines up several miles away for the first pass. Depending on which way the wind is blowing determines when the spray is turned on and off. The flaggers are always on the upwind side of the field so that they won't be sprayed during the application. On each succeeding pass the flagger moves one swath measure by pacing or a wheel calibrated for the necessary swath. When the application is completed the flaggers leave and a trim pass is applied the each end of the field. At times several passes of trim may be required depending on the field shape and obstructions. On the last pass the aircraft is headed back to the load truck as directly as possible landing for another load. If another aircraft is on the ground and loading but near take off the pilot will turn on the work lights and the inbound pilot will circle and give way. Sometimes the airstrip is so small that there is little room for two airplanes and the load truck. More recently the chaser goes to the field and clears it and then leaves with no flaggers left behind. Some new pesticide regulations require that no persons are present during the application. Now the pilot has to find the field on his own and he lines up on one edge of the field and on crossing the corner he punches a button on the GPS flagger that signifies the "A" point. At the completion of the swath run he punches "B". He then turns towards the far corner of the field and begins a swath and punches "C". From then on the lights on the bar mounted on the front of the aircraft in pilot view outside the cockpit will show the center of the next succeeding swath with three green vertical lights, with dots left and right of center to indicate distance off center. The enhanced accuracy of the new systems allows holding to approximately plus or minus one foot. No flaggers are required and irregular shapes are easily accommodated. Work production goes up about 30 percent with the GPS flagger simply because the pilot doesn't have to wait to set up fields and a host of other reasons. It is not uncommon to repeat the process for each load 25 to 50 times a day or working session. It is nearly as much work to set up for one load as for ten. Much has been done in the last few years to decease the number of people in the field and speed up the already fast application process.   The paperwork and regulations are beginning to take more time than the application although most of the required country paperwork is computerized and automated. Much the same procedure is followed for dry work like fertilizer, granules, and baits except the truck for loading has a large bucket mounted on a hydraulic ram that allows a ton or a ton and a half of material to be loaded by positioning the bucket over the hopper and tripping the lever to dump the load into the hopper via a lid in the top. This requires two loaders and a specially modified truck. Everything has to be specially bonded top prevent sparks in the case of sulfur dust applications or other potentially explosive materials. One loader stands on the wing and the other positions the load truck bucket over the hopper. When in position over the open hopper, the load is dumped into the aircraft. This type of loading is usually done with the engine idling. Fuel is usually added after the load is in and the hopper lid is shut.

Chapter Fourteen
The Struggle to Survive Retirement

I knew that things were on the down hill run when I noticed that the man I had worked for and with for years no longer waited for me to come to work. Usually we would discuss the days work and maps and go out to the parked planes together. Now when I came in, my maps would be laying on the desk and my former partner, now boss, was long gone to work. To add to the separation we flew entirely different types of aircraft so they didn't mix well in the same fields and we no longer flew as a team but as separate individuals. We had been splitting the hazardous fields so that each shared the risk but now I got nearly all the small dangerous and difficult fields. I could see that he was burning out from all the problems of the spraying business. It wasn't long before I found out he was trying to sell the business and there was no offer to sell to me so I could see the handwriting on the wall, I was going to be unemployed soon. They say the best laid plans go astray and so did mine. I needed two more years at my present income to pay off my mortgage and my savings would not be adequate to pay it off, the bottom line was I still was going to work during my so called retirement. When the new young owner showed up, he supposedly had Ag flying time but after watching him fly I knew he was going to need a lot of luck to make it in this business. I had broken in several pilots and I instinctively knew that this guy didn't have the right stuff. Only a couple of weeks into his assumption of the business he ran out of gas during an application and landed in a soft field and totaled the airplane, lucky for him he was not hurt. So now we were out a dry airplane which meant that each time we got a dry job we had to take a liquid sprayer apart and add a spreader for one or two loads and then take it off and clean the aircraft of dry material. No matter how well it was cleaned small pieces of dry material would clog the nozzles and require cleaning constantly during an application. I hated flying sulfur dust, beside being flammable and explosive, the stuff burned your eyes for days after an application and your pillow smelled like a box of matches no matter how many showers you took. I wouldn t have guessed it but my last load in the job of crop dusting would be a load of sulfur dust on melons. I knew the money had changed hands and a new younger pilot was being trained to take my place. It was time for me to go so at the end of the month, the end of the day, I laid my keys on the desk and asked the secretary to mail my last check to my home. I picked up my helmet, walked to my truck, and drove down the dirt road from the airport that I had traveled night and day for seventeen years. The was no gold watch, not even a thank you, I was out on the street once again. The feeling I had was like loosing my job, getting divorced, and having your dog die all on the same day. With my new found freedom, after being on call 24/7 for nearly 24 years, I was to say the least disoriented. Out of work, I looked for a job with another operation, but each one I looked at was a disaster area, poorly maintained aircraft, primitive mixing conditions and equipment. I tried to go to work for one of our competitors that were flying turbines. My spirits soared momentarily as I was hired, allowed to checkout in the turbine air tractor, something was amiss because I wasn't getting any work to do. It finally dawned on me that some financial doings were In the mill, and I wasn't needed any more, so I headed off down the road to the next adventure... I was so used to going to work, I didn't know how to live a life outside work. I had planned to go to Oshkosh, Wisconsin for the annual Experimental Aircraft Association Fly In. For all those years I dreamed of going with my friends except I was strapped to a big yellow bird spraying cotton. When I finally got there some years later it was a big disappointment. It turned out to be a giant sales pitch for mostly very wealthy people. Now over sixty years old, there were long hikes to anywhere the seminars were located.and there was no shuttle transportation from the outlying campgrounds. I was excited about volunteering until a snotty EAA employee dulled my enthusiasm. I volunteered and was taken to the tractor tram operation. When I walked in, the young EAA staffer asked "what are you doing here?", I replied that I had come to volunteer for whatever was available. I was told to wait outside, and since it was raining, I found a dry spot and waited. Pretty soon all around mounted up on the tractors and trams and drove away, briefed and mission in sight. I still waited, finally I realized I wasn't needed and left. It's kind of funny, six months later, I got a volunteer patch and a nice letter thanking me for volunteering. While walking around the displays of warbirds, my wife was tiring of walking in the heat and oppressive humidity, when I spotted an approaching tram. At that point I didn't care where it was going as long as we didn't have to walk. My wife and I accidentally boarded a private tour flight line tram or so we were informed by some passengers, we tried to get attention to get off with out any success, so when it slowed to near a stop we stepped off, and were immediately chewed out by another EAA "biggie". By now, it seems as though where ever I go, I'm not on the right side of this operation. For years I had read about the friendship and camaraderie at the EAA event, but from where I stood, something was lacking. I didn't see any President or Officers riding around in cut down Volkswagens, they were all in large SUV's with air conditioning and darkly tinted windows. Although we had paid our fees and were members we were not allowed to go into the museum a day or two early when the crowds were thin and we could park near the entrance. My wife had a heart condition and we later had to park across a busy street and run across it to hoof it up a hill to the building. We noticed that foreign visitors were quickly escorted into the building with great pomp and circumstance on the days before we were allowed. Once inside, the museum was wonderful a collection of warbirds, aerobatic aircraft, and lots of history, but not a single crop dusting airplane.

The airplanes that fed a nation, put salad on your table, cotton in your underwear, and other farm products for many, many, years were absent. They were probably smart, who wants a clunky, smelly, airplane, that leaks chemical on the floor in a museum? Not even a mention... so much for fame and glory. I am glad I went once after waiting all those years, but I won't miss standing in line for substandard food, the insufferable humid heat, and the crowds jamming everything from showers to outhouses. Zsa Zsa Gabor once said "too much of a gud thing is Vunderful", I don't think so. One morning when I was jogging with a friend around the island formed by the construction of the London Bridge and felt a strange chill. When I got home I felt like I had a royal case of the flu. For the next few days I continued to feel worse and finally couldn't do much but go to the bathroom and bed. I went to a clinic and the news wasn't good. They decided I had pneumonia. They gave me anti-biotics and the x-rays showed dark spots on my lungs. So I rested and took medication and did everything I could think of to shake the malady. It didn't shake. Each time I went in for an x-ray it looked the same. For a while I thought they were just copying the old ones. I took a special medication given to aids patients for pneumonia, it still held on. The people at the clinic suggested an expensive diagnostic procedure($2500) was needed and of course I had no insurance. I realized at that point that after surviving years of crop dusting at night and flying of all sorts I might not survive this time. I had a doctor friend that told me in a very nice way that there wasn't much they could do except wait. It was now too late to go to Oshkosh my dream for many years. So, another dream was to ride the Durango Silverton Narrow Gauge Railroad in Colorado. I wasn't feeling any better so I suggested to my wife, "you know I could just sit here and wait to die or I could go to Durango and ride the train, if I'm gonna die I may as well die in Durango".. So we hooked up the travel trailer and headed east. When we got to Durango it was raining, really raining, with land slides and the whole thing. We made reservations and waited three days to board the train at a nearby trailer camp. We finally boarded the train and I don't know if it was the train or the trees but I began to feel better and pretty soon it was business as usual, my health returned miraculously without explanation. We traveled around that summer to the beach and elsewhere and when I returned home I had to find work. Finding a job over age sixty is no easy project. Despite my education and ratings I have now reached the gray ceiling. The letters say I don't fit their profile for the job, but it is another way to say we only hire the young. I got some financial backing from a previous employer and friend and bought a hangar and set up an aircraft repair business that required my work 12 hours a day six days a week. The wind blew dirt there constantly, and it was hotter than Hades during the summer and colder than the artic in the winter. It was nearly a two hour round trip from home so the day extended to 14 hours. After a year of spinning my wheels and trading dollars I decided to throw in the towel. The hangar was sold, I lost my investment and now was unemployed again. I pick up work from private individuals when I can, but with the sliding economy it is dwindling to nearly nothing. Especially after the 9/11 debacle. The local airport has criminalized me and others by requiring us to work for a Fixed Base Operator, and they will not issue a business license unless I have a lease on the airport. So, all my ratings are not of much use now. The pilot ratings because of age and the mechanic's because of the city fathers. So I bootleg, working clandestinely in people's hangars, hauling my tools around in my truck like a gypsy outlaw with his wagon.

Chapter Fifteen
Sixteen-Hundred Miles
In An Open Cockpit Biplane

The internet is a dangerous place. A friend called and said he had seen a small biplane in an ad, and asked if I wanted to go back east a pick it up. I like to bring dreams to people. It had been quite a while since I had flown anything, so when the opportunity to fly a two place open cockpit biplane from Cleveland, Ohio to Lake Havasu City, Arizona presented it self, I thought it would be a great adventure. I didn't really get to prepare or think about it I just packed a bag and went to Las Vegas, Nevada to catch a commercial flight to Cleveland. It took all day from early in the morning to drive to Las Vegas, get checked in, go through security, and finally wait for the departure with a stop and layover at Chicago Midway. When I got there, Cleveland was humming and it was near midnight before I collapsed into a motel near the airport. Since they were three hours ahead of my home, morning came very early. I probably got four hours sleep. I called the fellow with the biplane and he came and picked me up. When we arrived at the airport, the little red biplane was hunkered down in one corner like an elderly dog waiting to go out and pee. Bright red and silver, it had four ailerons and two cockpits with a sliding canopy on the rear cockpit. I looked it over carefully as possible under the circumstances and then looked at the logbooks. The previous owner had done most of the right things and recorded the necessary information. He omitted a few critical details, some of which he may not have been aware of. The aircraft sported a new wood prop which should have been a warning. The pilot handbook cautioned "100 mph on approach minimum" I knew little about the airplane and its tricks, but I was going to learn soon. The workmanship was good and the present owner was 79 years old and he had last flown it 6 months ago, he also mentioned that he only had flown it with an instructor on board. The cockpit was large enough for the prospective owner and anxious to get under way I gave him

99

the check, he gave me the bill of sale, and necessary paper work and I loaded up my bag, did a preflight, and climbed in. With a lot of tail dragger experience under my belt, I felt no intimidation as I turned the key to start its engine. It ran smoothly as I taxied out, while the ex owners wife videotaped my progress toward the runway. I could not see anything forward as the biplanes nose stuck straight up in front of me blocking any forward view. Both windshields were tinted and limited the view forward. With a radio call and a clearing turn for traffic I taxied out on the runway and applied the power slowly dancing ever so gently on the rudder pedals to maintain control. The rudder was super sensitive compared to anything I had flown before, even the frisky Luscombe was tame in comparison. When I lifted off, the biplane was incredibly pitch sensitive bucking and bouncing with every wind current. The smallest movement of the stick caused the ailerons to roll the wings at a high rate of speed. There were no ball bearings in the control bell cranks so the control stick seemed to stick in whatever position I moved it, requiring me to constantly re-center each control input. I braced my arm on my leg to stop the convulsions and soon had both hands on the stick braced against my legs to quiet the violent excursions. I had flown RC model airplanes that were tail heavy, and this aircraft had all the earmarks of tail heavy. Things were beginning to come together. I realized the new wood prop was there because it was a cheaper replacement for the metal one that once resided there, also weighing about twenty pounds less. With no one occupying the front pit of course it was tail heavy. The aircraft had to be flown with the canopy back for takeoff and landing so that was a few more pounds slid aft. My first landing was of concern because the pilots operating handbook stated that a 100 mph should be maintained on the approach, the rate of descent at that speed was awesome, and sure to make my hair stand up with out command. I got down ok without any problems. My first stop was less than sixty miles and when I landed there were gliders active across the field but no one in evidence near

100

the gas truck. After walking around a bit, I decided to go a few miles north to another strip and landed. Again, no one was around. After I sat a while, deciding what to do a fellow appeared from nowhere and asked if I needed fuel. Refueled I headed for the next stop. By now, I had damped my control inputs to the point where I could fly with one hand. However, the little biplane was still incredibly wild in pitch. The pilots operating handbook also stated that the boost pump should be on when the fuel was down to 8 gallons or less. This would be a longer leg and I did not know how much fuel the engine was burning with only one stop so I flew for about an hour and fifteen minutes. I had enough fuel for two hours (I thought) and arriving at the destination, I circled the field looking for the windsock to choose a runway into the wind. I had called the Unicomm frequency to ask the wind condition but got no answer, with the wind blasting around and through the cockpit, I am not sure I could hear it anyway. I tried putting my head down in the cockpit to reduce the noise and it helped some. Paralleling one runway I felt the engine miss a beat or two then hesitate a bit as though running out of fuel I knew I had at least 8 gallons remaining so I turned on the fuel boost pump and the engine immediately died as though the mixture was pulled full lean. I turned the boost off and made a diving turn 180 degrees to the available runway crosswind, at that point the engine began to run again. When I touched down all was well at first but the crosswind required a bit more input than I had so even though all three wheels were on the ground and the stick full aft a gust started the tail-heavy beast into a ground loop. Making a big circle with one tip dragging and a few hops later, I came to a halt with a small patch on the left wing scrapped and a broken wheel half but still able to taxi. At this point, I thought it was a good time to stop for the day. I put the red beast in at hangar and started to work. I inspected the aircraft closely and the only damage appeared to be the small fabric patch about 3 inches in diameter and the broken wheel half. I had not noticed before, but a gas tank vent made its exit near the axle of the left wheel facing aft, drawing a vacuum on the fuel tank. I added a piece of hose to the line and faced it forward so it would pressurize the tank. Next, I needed nose weight, I borrowed an old battery from one of the operators for the weight but I was afraid of the fire danger if it still had some juice. (It was supposed to be dead). I found a coat hangar in the hangar and momentarily touched it to the terminals while holding it with pliers. The coat hangar glowed red immediately, not a good idea to carry it like that. Someone suggested I buy a couple of rubber coated barbells at Wal Mart and I did along with some duct tape. I added about thirty pounds of weight to the motor mount. A fellow at a sky diving school had an old Cessna with a blown engine and he offered to let me use a wheel for the trip. With the wheel and nose weight installed I test flew it the next morning and it was a completely different airplane, at least flyable without convulsions. I continued the flight cross-country and began to enjoy the scenery. I made my gas stops an hour or less and the engine ran like a sewing machine with no problems. East of St. Louis, Missouri I dodged thunderstorms, I sat for hours watching weather and the storms three hundred and fifty miles long, seemed to be stalled without moving so I took off and headed south to skirt the storms. I had done well flight planning to this point but one of my gas stops I planned on lacked one important detail, the runway was marginal for this machine, and I missed it. Setting up the approach, I undershot and flared and though I touched down right on the threshold it took most of the runway to stop without the use of brakes. I was a little more careful on the next selection paying more attention to the runway length. One I picked indicated a 6000-foot runway, when I got there only half was available as they were repaving it. Everywhere I went the people of the USA were so helpful and kind. Can you imagine that someone, a stranger, would take a wheel off his airplane and offer it to you, with the condition, "Send it back when you get though". People loaned me tools, hangars, cars, and fed me all across the US all without charge or expectation of return. One fellow, operating a gyro school came down the taxiway with a piece of cinnamon toast and a cup of coffee and said "I thought you needed this to get you started." The plains were one thing but the terrain began to rise out west. As I flew higher, I discovered the little biplane was underpowered for the weight and drag it was hauling around, and the propeller was over pitched so that the engine could not develop full power. Now in addition to the high approach and landing speed it took a long runway to get it to flying speed. I removed the air filter element to get an extra hundred rpm and finally at Albuquerque I emptied the airplane of all but essential weight and shipped the stuff by ground to my home. In some areas, the climb rate was near zero with full throttle so I resorted to soaring the windward slopes to gain altitude to get by some areas of high terrain. In some instances, I had to divert several miles off course to get enough altitude to keep going west. Downdrafts would cause my stomach to drop to my knees and there was deep concern that I might not make it. There were more rocks and rough ground than I remembered from my last ferry flight over this same area especially since I was getting a much closer view than I ever had before. By the time I got to Holbrook, Arizona, I had covered sixteen hundred miles, most of the time below a thousand feet above the ground. A couple of times I passed by radio towers a hundred feet below their tops. It sure made my hair stand on end even though I had plenty of clearance. On my arrival at Holbrook, I thought I would make a quick fuel stop and be home that day. After fueling and taking off for Winslow, I had been warned that the airport may have an operating tower because of the forest fires nearby, I could hear them talking to the tankers working the fires and when I called for a clearance I was informed it was IFR due to smoke, and only a mile visibility. Because of the low visibility and no instrument equipment in the tiny biplane, I returned to Holbrook. I parked it in the hangar and took a truck ride home to return when the smoke and weather cleared. It is now July and really hot and the density altitude makes take offs and landings in the little beast hazardous at best. I flight planned for several days and rested. The owner I was flying for decided it was time to pull the wings and trailer it the rest of the way home. He never asked me to help or even mentioned that he was going. I chalked it all up to ignorance. Mine and his. Mine because I risked my life to bring a dream home for someone that didn't appreciate it. I didn't charge him a penny, and he reneged on his promise to allow me to fly Young Eagles (kids who have never flown before). And his for not asking the important questions about the aircraft that he later objected to. He bought the aircraft sight unseen and with no way to negotiate the sale, I had to fly it home and basically be a test pilot for an aircraft we knew nothing about. Well, I learned and pronto, but it didn't make the trip any easier. Flight planning the remainder of the trip would have been hazardous at best because of the limited performance and restricted range. I had not slept well on the trip, flight planning morning and night and watching the weather channel endlessly and the occasional Doppler radar display for thunderstorms. Along the way, nearly every stop had a computer hooked to weather and menu driven it was easy to use and gave me a lot of info in a hurry. It was reassuring to know the wind and weather conditions at every stop along the way via this device. The little biplane was fun in spite of its problems. I discovered that wearing a cloth helmet allowed the sun to burn your forehead, your eyelids, your lips, and your forearms. I had a heavy clipboard in the cockpit to hold my map and all the necessary info for airport arrival and departure. I found it impossible to fold a map in an open cockpit in flight. I wrote down all the necessary details of height, frequency, and runway numbers on a 3 by 5 card. Another terror came in the form of a message on my GPS receiver. "Batteries Low". Although I was still navigating by map, compass, and time, the GPS made the trip a lot easier but with low batteries, it meant I had to change them in flight. My particular unit requires removing the bottom like a clip on a handgun. The batteries are then pushed out and dumped like cartridges on the floor in a plastic basket I had under the seat. I wear glasses for distance, but not reading, so I had to look under them for the polarity of the batteries marked in barely visible writing in the plastic (I should have marked the positive ends with red paint) all the while holding the stick carefully so the airplane would not pitch or dive while my attention was diverted elsewhere. I also had to constantly S turn everywhere I went because the front cockpit windshield, wing struts, and wires obscured forward vision. There is not much baggage capacity because little or no weight can be carried behind the pilot without changing the flight characteristics. I carried most of my gear in a bag strapped in with the front seat belts and harness. It was quite a trip all things considered. Would I do it again? Probably not. I am terribly proud to be an American, the people of this country are kind, generous, and helpful to a degree you cannot imagine unless you take a trip such as this one. I am only sorry I could not take someone with me to share the trip, but looking back it is probably too great a risk to share with an unsuspecting passenger. I do not mind sticking my neck out, but doing it for someone else is another thing altogether. It was a trip I will not soon forget, and hopefully I will not forget the lessons I have learned in the process. After my return, the owner of the biplane left it disassembled in the hangar and has not flown since I returned. Imagine risking your life to bring someone a dream, and then have them throw the dream in the trash. After all the thousands of hours flying and all the ratings I have gained, I am still a student pilot. I am still learning. I am ready for my next adventure.

Chapter Sixteen
The Next Adventure

Since I have been working on my own, I have worked on several interesting airplanes. At one time I worked on several Cessna 185 amphibians. The floats on these aircraft require nearly as much maintenance as the entire airplane and engine. Corrosion is always a problem. Major maintenance or replacement of struts requires a heavy overhead hoist to remove and replace the wheels and floats. I like to work on the older planes, and I have taken a liking to fabric work. I have tried to build my own airplane from a kit or from scratch having failed to complete either, it is still a far off goal. I have become involved in the Experimental Aircraft Association at the chapter level. With all the years of experience flying and fixing, I hope to be able to contribute some useful information to beginners and hopefuls in the process of building aircraft at home. If all goes well I hope to build my own aircraft. It really doesn't matter if I finish it before I leave this world, it's the dream that matters. I still build and fly radio controlled model airplanes. To date I have built and flown a C130 Hercules, a Ford Tri-Motor, and a Douglas A26, along with countless other glider, aerobatic, and scale aircraft. I will probably never fly the full scale equivalent of these aircraft so this is as close as I can get. Along the way I have helped several people restore old airplanes, build experimentals, and I have test flown several different types of aircraft and helicopters. With a day off I nearly always end up at an airfield or model airstrip. The majority of the people there are mostly my family and it always feels like home. Before my Mom died, she gave me a little ceramic boat that sums it up nicely. On the bottom is the following: "Some day your ship with come in, and with your luck, you'll probably be at the airport". My Crop dusting license in California expires this month, this year. Because of bureaucratic meddling, it probably won't be renewed this year. The end of the Bug Killers reign of terror is coming to a close. There are new disciplines to learn, and new places to go, and new people to meet. All of us chasing the sky. It's another adventure, another dream, and I can hardly wait to see what's going to happen next.

Chapter Seventeen
North of the Border

It turns out that the next adventure came in the form of an invitiation. A friend needed a Piper PA 12 Super Cruiser moved from Creston, British Columbia in Canada to Lake Havasu City, Arizona. I had flown a lot of east west stuff but never north to south across the western US. I started my flight planning on the EAA website on the internet and finished by studying sectional and wac charts to get familiar with the route. By the time the day of departure arrived I had a pretty good idea of the terrain and the weather forecast. Early AM we left in a Lancair Super ES powered by a Continental IO-550 and headed north. This is a state of the art homebuilt aircraft with fixed landing gear that can carry four people over two hundred miles per hour for more distance than my bladder can travel. It was very hot in the desert when we left and now it was getting cold as we approached Hawthorne, Nevada. We landed and I wasted little time in getting long pants and jacket on before the next departure. We then headed for Redmond, Oregon, the site of the Lancair Factory and the Lancair Yearly Fly In. We spent a day there and then headed for PortHill, Idaho a small grass strip on the Canadian border. After a day there looking around a friend, "Uncle Jerry" and I, prepared to launch the PA12 Super Cruiser south. This was to be the first ride from north to south across the USA. I have flown many times east west and I knew it pretty well, but this was really different. The mountains, rivers, and valleys set a picture of unending vistas of water, green and brown as far as the eye could see. Many hours we spent cruising a hundred feet above the terrain, many hours spent thousands of feet above the rivers, streams, and deserts. I didn't realize how tired I was till our next to last gas stop. I wanted to get to our over night stop and get some rest. After refueling I miscalculated when sundown was and as we neared our destination I realized it was going to be dark, very dark. The airplane didn't have landing lights and our arrival at the overnight stop was more of a thump than a landing and we taxied the airplane to the parking area with the use of a flashlight. The next morning we returned to our home field. Fourteen hours were recorded in the logbook for this trip.

Chapter Eighteen
An Old Friend Revisited

Banjo fancied himself a tail dragger pilot. Most of his flying time was spent in tricycle gear aircraft. He not only wanted to fly a tail dragger, he wanted to buy a Swift...for the uninitiated the Swift represents one of the more demanding conventional geared aircraft a pilot can lay his hand to. Especially with a higher horsepower engine and constant speed prop. I agreed to take on the task of teaching him to fly, but first he had to master the Cub with 135 horsepower. It didn't take long before he had made himself comfortable in the Cub and he finalized the sale of a pristine 1946 Globe Swift. On the day of delivery I was to test fly the Swift before the sale. It had been a long time since I flew mine with 145 horse power, the one in transit was a 180 horsepower aircraft with a constant speed propeller. Like an old friend my take off and landing were a labor of love. The Swift falling to hand like an old leather glove worn many times. We had a great time learning the Swift all over again. Burning seven gallons an hour and cruising 130 knots it is still one of the most delightful small aircraft in existence. It does exactly what you want it to and nothing more or less. The visibility is outstanding and the seat comfortable. We launched to Jackson, California for the National Swift fly in and in four hours landed in the middle of several of the most beautiful old airplanes ever made. We saw old friends and made new ones and just enjoyed all the old airplanes and people. After the trip home I decided to buy an airplane to restore. It came to me from a monthly circular in the form of a Taylorcraft L2A. A little world war two observation aircraft in which the rear seat rotated 180 degrees allowing the observer to see artillery targets facing aft. A small desk was in the back for marking maps. Powered by a little 65 horsepower Continental engine, it had wood spars and wood ribs, and mechanical brakes. I worked many hours cleaning and painting and assembling parts, I spent ten hours of research for every hour I worked on it and all in spare time. Which is to say, not much. I could see that I didn't have time or the money to restore the little bird to it's original form so I advertised it in the same place and sold it to a retired airline pilot in possession of both. Another dream down the drain. I started looking for another dream the next day. In the meantime a friend, "Irish" had bought a homebuilt kit amphibian and I lent a hand in getting it ready to fly. It was supposed to be nearly completed and ready to fly but a year or more later it still had problems. We just kept doggedly sorting and fixing. In the meantime the learning curve was getting shorter and shorter. The day finally came when it was ready to fly, and yours truly was the test pilot. Fix and fly became the order of the day. The airplane was stored for a long time and many of the installation details were in error and needed correction. We finally got all the details completed. The flight test program continued till we got the required hours flown off so I could give the owner dual instruction in his now completed aircraft. Later we had a difficult time with the sea trials so the owner elected to sell his prized aircraft. It flew from Arizona to Florida and now resides there.

Chapter Nineteen
Another Biplane

Another day, another phone call. "High Dollar", the owner of a Stearman biplane, called to say his engine had thrown a rod after takeoff and he was able to dead stick land the airplane without a scratch. Some pilot I have to say. I thought from my ag experience that it would take three days. One to take it off, one to clean and repair, and one to put it back on. As I began to disassemble the engine for removal the owner inquired if we could powder coat, paint and polish the many parts of the engine and airframe. Months later we finally put the last bolt and finishing touches on the lovely old biplane. To my surprise "High Dollar" wanted me to test fly it. He was smarter than I thought. I had gobs of tailwheel time but it had been over twenty years since I had flown a Stearman, and most of that in much higher powered models. To say my blood pressure was up a bit would be an understatement. Taxiing out, the biplane seemed much larger that I remembered and the engine ran much smoother due to many modifications including better bearings and pistons. I pushed the throttle gently forward and off we went. Making a circuit around the field, all the pressures and temperatures were ok so I landed and thought the work was done. Then "High Dollar" flew, and later asked if I wanted to give rides in the Stearman biplane. So next thing I know I am being drug tested, insured, and making advertising materials to get the ball rolling. I rebuilt a set of old boarding steps from a defunct airline that fit perfectly up to the trailing edge of the wing. I built a tow bar to make it easy to move the Stearman, and the "High Dollar" had a spare golf cart that I modified with a hitch on the front to make moving the Stearman in and out of the hangar easier. All painted bright yellow. I got some coveralls and started a career flying rides in a biplane at age 68. A wide variety of people came to fly in the big yellow machine. Some for their birthday, some for their first open cockpit ride. A few hugs later I was having fun working for peanuts flying and maintaining the old Stearman. She was built in 1942 in Wichita,

Kansas by the Boeing Aircraft Company. She served as an Army trainer for the duration of the war, then was mustered out by the Reconstruction Finance Company to a company called Continental Dusters, the parent of the now Delta Air Lines. Many years later it was restored and painted in Navy colors, all yellow with color bands. Of course it was up dated to better radios and pretty much all new everything else that needed attention. Still a nice flying old bird, everyone that sees her thinks she's pretty. She had been in the military, served as a duster, and ended up flying rides, just like me.

Chapter Twenty
TLC

I have to stop reading circulars. I found another airplane to replace the Taylorcraft. In a remote desert strip it sat forlorn and in need of work but still flying. Like most aircraft I have purchased, you don't really know what you have until you start to take it apart. So the money changed hands and I flew it home knowing it was going to need work. That's when the fun begins... The engine ran well but the landing gear was missing some parts and someone had installed a stack of washers so it would sit level. Two springs were missing to keep the axles from bottoming out on bumps and hard landings. I spent many hours fixing small details but managed to keep it flying and fun. I gave anybody that came near a ride. What a hoot, all sorts of folks, old and young, loved the little airplane. It mostly just chugged around locally, with an occaisional cross country flight. I got all prepared to take a trip across the US to Oshkosh, Wisconsin to the EAA fly in. "Irish" the great guy I worked with on the seaplane, now wanted to make the trek back east. He had some change in plans and moved away from the area so that dream vaporized, many do. It takes a lot of planning to make a flight in a simple airplane. It lacks power for some flights, it is slow, much like a tree house that moves ever so slowly. It is however, very comfortable to sit and fly in for long periods of time. On the last trip across the US it was a matter of up early to fly and then wait out the thunderstorms in the afternoon.

It's not much different now, except the weather is becoming much more violent. The use of GPS is becoming widespread and it makes cross country navigation and planning light years easier than yesterdays use of beacons, VOR, and dead reckoning.

Chapter 21
Dreams and things….

I try to help people realize their dreams by making them mine. This year my health and energy is declining. I am working on three dreams at once. The first dream is a project rising out of eight years of hard work. It is a bush airplane, all metal, with a large Lycoming engine. Countless parts and details go into putting an aircraft together. Many people assist in bringing a machine like this into the air. Some mechanical, some composites, some electrical, and others that help to troubleshoot things that don't work. A homebuilt airplane is a huge bunch of compromises, and in some cases the builder must design, or determine function and make it work, and eventually fly. In the end it will come down to the first flight. Some adjustments may be necessary but there is always the unknown, that's why they have test pilots. In this case that would be me. The second dream is also many years in the making. Another homebuilt replica of the Piper Super Cub with many improvements over the original. Fabric covered it is a throw back to the days when airplanes had a tailwheel, and like the others, it has to be moulded and shaped like a clay vessel, a product of the hands. Friends and coffee, and endless hours of drilling and fixing to make things work. This too will have to be test flown to determine airworthiness….The people involved are expert craftsmen, they love their work, and pride and attention to detail is meticulous. I feel like a midwife assisting the birth or yet another flying machine, born of a dream, built with the hands. The third dream is less tangible. I helped "Irish" to build his dream airplane and during the test flying he developed an illness of the type scattered about the minefield of old age. He dreamed of flying it back to

Oshkosh, Wisconsin for the National Annual fly in. Without a lengthy explanation, the aircraft was sold and the dream went with it. So, because I had an old airplane that needed flying I was going to fly him to Oshkosh, to fulfill the dream of another time and place...my own minefield looms ahead and I must honor Carpe Diem, so at last the Bugkiller becomes the Dream Catcher, not a bad job for retirement....

Chapter 22
Personal Effects

I expected to not be able to fly this year. I had made up my mind to give up flying for good. Like the addict giving up his prized possession, I dreaded the end of having a flight at will. But I still can't predict the future. As I trekked into the doctor's office, I was trying to decide how I would cope with the failure to pass my FAA medical flight exam for second class. Marching through the steps to the exam, each was passed, and I began to feel my blood pressure subside. Lo, and behold I passed with no restrictions. Even my eyes passed the test, which would normally require a wavier for distant vision. Fate has played yet another hand in my poker game of life. So now, no excuses, I have sold my beloved Citabria, expecting to lose my medical, and now I am planeless. I am back to looking for another airplane to fly. It's a surprise. Back to the internet, I found an all metal orphan called a Pazmany PL1. Named after its designer, it is an all metal two place side by side trainer designed for homebuilders. The Taiwan government built 58 of them for trainers for their military pilots. Mildly aerobatic and equipped for IFR flight, they flew theirs from the right side, the brakes are on the right side only. On the one I have, the brakes are on the left. The visibility is great and it is fun to fly. A bit tight for the large, it fits my 70 inch 170 pound frame just right. Of course, it was far away. Flying from Las Vegas to North Carolina is an all day trip. I was going to make the trip solo, but I invited a co-pilot to go along. "Uncle Jerry" is one of the "Great Generation". A Navy vet, he raised a family, worked at many businesses, and has traveled all over the world visiting nearly all the countries in existence at the time. When it was still possible, he flew all over the US and Central and South America piloting his own aircraft. We both looked forward to the upcoming trip across this beautiful country without landing at a single tower controlled airport. A freedom few others can enjoy. Leaving at daybreak, with all the various

117

security and other delays, we finally arrived about one thirty in the morning in Jacksonville, NC. The next morning the owner "Hook" took us out to see the airplane and fly it. It looked good and flew well, so we exchanged money and paper and were airborne about noon, westbound. Flying under a scattered overcast for a while we did not land at any tower controlled airports. We could have, but we were barnstorming, "Uncle Jerry and Me". At each well kept airport, we found friendly mom and pops everywhere we went. The national gas price average seemed to be near five dollars per gallon of gas. This translates to very expensive flying by any measure. When we got to Arkansas, we spent a couple of days heads down waiting for tornados to pass. When the weather cleared, we were airborne for nearly thirteen hours, attempting to put as much distance between us and "tornado alley" as we could. The strongest winds we encountered were at Lake Havasu Arizona, a sixty degree crosswind at thirty five knots….we made it down ok. My next trip is to ferry a Murphy Super Rebel homebuilt to central Idaho. An adventure created by the need to move an airplane eight years in the building to it's new home. "Wafflebutt" started it in San Diego, CA and then moved it to the desert to finish. Countless hours and many rivets and parts later it was ready to fly. I didn't intend to fly it initially but during a taxi test to lift the tail at speed the aircraft lifted itself airborne and began to fly. It flew well, but there are always small details that need fixing, so it is fly, fix, fly fix, until all the problems are solved. Our first try to ferry the aircraft was stalled by rain then snow, then mud. On the second try, "Uncle Jerry" and me lifted off at daybreak and headed north. During the climb in the hot desert air, the oil temperature hovered dangerously near the red line. There is a lot to do initially on a flight of this type so my attention was scanning all possibilities. At one point I nearly aborted the flight but the temp dropped ten degrees as we leveled off at cruise altitude of 8500 feet. "Uncle" flew while I navigated, checked fuel management, and watched the gauges nervously. I was flying eight years of a man's life and I

118

didn't want to make any mistakes that could cost him his prize. Flying over the Nevada desert is like flying over the moon. Lotsa nothing. As you approach Twin Falls, Idaho, things get green, and mountains and valleys are every where. Refueling at Mountain Home we headed north to our final destination. At altitude, thoughts eventually turn to the rugged inaccessibility of the terrain. An engine failure here would be a costly and probably terminal endeavor. About fifty miles out, a large thunderstorm loomed ahead and stuff was building west of us so decided to go between them. At one point a lightning bolt struck about a half mile in front of us so I did a 90 degree to the left and then went around the storms without further problems. Our descent into Elk City revealed a panorama of green and trees. The airstrip is shaped like a hockey stick. We made a couple of passes and when we turned in for landing the oil temperature was threatening to touch red once again so we committed to landing. We flared and turned to follow the strip and landed. As we taxied in we were greeted by a happy builder, owner 'Wafflebutt". Wafflebutt, Uncle, and Major GB shot skeet, rode ATV's, laughed a lot, and ate too much. Time to go home, we mounted a pickup truck and headed to Boise, then Las Vegas by air, then rental car home the end of a great adventure...... The end of most men's lives is signaled by someone giving the last remaining objects in their possession to their widow or family. It's not much to show for a lifetime. In my dad's case it was a wallet, a set of keys, some pocket change. In my case, it won't be much different. , I was fortunate enough to be free to fly most of my life, it was reward enough for a guy without a degree, nearly legally blind when I started flying. Unable to get a flying job because I wore glasses, I ended up where they didn't care. Cropdusting, a bug killer at best, thousands of hours close to the ground, at night, in the heat of the desert, A cropduster's life....

119

Chapter 23
The Final Chapter

Dealing with the minefield of old age we stepped on one. My friend of more than fifty years, my wife, was parking the car in the garage in such a manner that I couldn't get past the car. I had a ping pong ball hanging from the ceiling so all one had to do was guide the car so the antenna touched the ball, presto, just the right position for maximum clearance. But it wasn't happening and I thought it was just carelessness due to fatigue, it wasn't. Later I noticed that she had difficulty operating the tv controller. Then she was unable to set the thermostat. Things were being lost left and right. She began to gesture to people on tv thinking they could see her. Sometimes lucid, I tried to make the best of it till returning home from a trip, she began to exhibit even more bizarre behavior. I began to research on the net and found all sorts of information which it turns out, I wasn't paying attention to. The signs were all there, dementia was in the beginning stages. Some people began to notice the changes, the weight loss, and the obvious aging of a once lovely and athletic woman. I resigned myself to the different person, and went to support groups. The information they shared was really more than I wanted to know. I reluctantly scheduled a visit to a neurologist who had given a seminar on dementia I previously attended. We waited two weeks for an appointment, then an hour past the time we were admitted. The doctor spent15 minutes asking questions, then excused himself and returned with a hand full of sample drugs "to smooth her moods". Of course she wouldn't take them. Good thing, I later found out they would have made her nauseous. I am asking questions everywhere from everyone. Is it a long term thing, how long? Don't know, what can we do? Drugs. No cure. My ability to fly, and work were seriously curtailed. I am a full time caregiver. I had offers from well meaning friends but it upset her terribly if I left. I tried to make plans to get day care if only for a limited time, but it was to no avail or to costly.

Living on social security, you don't hire nurses and skilled help for this situation. Our boat was floating along at least for a while until one morning there was blood in the toilet. She didn't want to go to the hospital, scared out of her wits by previous experiences . After several days, I could stand no more and forced her to the emergency room. After being miss diagnosed and given the wrong treatment for nearly thirteen hours, it was discovered that there was blood in her urine. Surgery scheduled, tumors were removed from her bladder and the biopsy sent to another hospital for a second opinion. They concurred, and the urologist indicated a surgery to remove the bladder and add a bag, along with chemo and radiation. Trying to explain this to a woman with dementia is like explaining the universe to a dog, the dog listens and love's you, but has no clue what you are talking about. One thing for sure she doesn't want to go to the hospital and repeat the former experience. Now the preparations begin for power of attorney, advance health directive, and other needs including hospice...no one seems to have answers for why, how long, where, when, and what happens if you don't. My son has a keen observation, it is easier to say than do when the end of days is in sight. So here I am writing the final chapter for her and possibly for me. Exposed to huge amounts of pesticide, the jury is still out for me, for now. I was never afraid for even a minute, flying the worst chemicals in the world over thousands of acres, not at night, not under power lines, not when I had engine failures, my pulse never moved a beat. But now the fear of what comes next wrenches my guts, tightens my throat, I wake up crying in the night, helpless to fight the fear of what comes next, not for me, for her. My own final chapter is near, now I have discovered there are worse things than crashing in an airplane, I am preparing to reach out my hand and touch the face of God.

121

Cessna A188 B AgWagon. Continental 10-520 285 HP.
A really good 175 gallon machine. Most have gone to
South America......

G164B AgCat 450 HP Pratt and Whitney my partner
Is aboard......

M18A Dromader 58 foot span, 600 gallon machine
With Russian KAD 1200HP derated to 987, ten foot
Four blade screw.

AT-301 Air Tractor over cotton, 600 HP Pratt and
Whitney, great 275 gallon machine.

StearCat 450 HP Stearman with four ailerons and
hard swing over canopy. Sulphur rig note spreader
Under belly.

Weatherly 201B 450 HP Pratt and Whitney

Sulphur Fire on AT-301 Air Tractor.

Swift GC1B 145 HP Continental 1946 vintage.

1946 Luscombe 8F 90 HP Continental.

Scratch built C130AHercules powered by
4 OS 40 FP's Brakes and operating rear cargo
door. 15 LBS. Fibreglass over balsa and foam.

AcroSport 2 Lycoming 0-320 150 HP.

Beechcraft Musketeer Sport (Mouse) 150
HP Lycoming. Our commuter airplane.

Aircraft Types
The following is a list of aircraft types I have flown.

A

Acrosport 2   0-320
Aeronca 7AC, 11AC, 15AC, 7ECA, 7GCCA
Aero Commander 260(Meyers)
Air Tractor 301, 302, 402
American Yankee/ 108, 150

B
Beech A23-19, B19, B23, B95, B55, C55, B55, D55,
   D35, E33, K35, M35, N35, S35, A36
Bell 47 G, Tomcat
Bellanca 14-19, 14-30A,
Blanik L13
Boeing A75 220, 450, 600

C

Cessna 120, 140, 150 0-200/0-320, 152, 170, 172,
   177, 180, 182, 185 amphib IO-520 Lyc TIO-540,
   A188B, 206 337, 414
Chinook(homebuilt ultralight test flights) 2 separate ac. +2

D

Douglas DC7C Copilot Jack Beadle PIC
Dromader M18A , M18

E

F

Fairchild M62C C220 (PT-23)

Fornier RF4DVW powered sailplane

Funk F23, Ag aircraft powered by a 390 Ford V8
(Gerschwander Conv)

G

Globe Swift GC1B 0-360 Lyc and C 145
Grumman G164B 450, Tiger, Lynx 150 AA1C

H

Hughes 269B, 500C
Hurricane Hauler (ultralight)

I

J

K

L

Lake LA 4
Lancair 360 180 HP,
Luscombe 8A, 8E, 8F

M

Mooney 180 hp Ranger, M20C
MU-13 German HP sailplane war prize on deck of
Canadian Destroyer
Murphy Super Rebel Lyc 0-540

N

Navion

O

P

Pazmany PL1 0-320
Piper PA-12, PA-18 90, 115, 135, 150, L21, PA20,
PA22 108/ 135/150/160 PA23-150, PA23-160,
PA 28-140, PA28-201TC 180, 235, PA32-260Pawnee 150
J3-65/85/150 (Canadian Ultralight)

Q

R

Rans Arial S15 tri gear

S

Searey Rotax turbo 115

Schwicher 2-33A sailplane

Stinson 10A

T

Thrush 600 S2R

Taylorcraft 65 hp

U

V

Van's RV-4, RV-6A

W

Weatherly 201B 450

X

Y

Z

Zodiac 601HD 0-200

To date 102 types 06-19-08

A History of My Model Sailboats (from 1992)
November 2004

I have three model sailboats which I built when I was twelve or thirteen years of age. The boats were built at Luther Burbank Junior High School in Highland Park, California. A model building class taught by Mr. Norman E. Hines met for about an hour a day, each week day. The boats were constructed for a competition sponsored by the Los Angeles Evening Herald-Examiner a Hearst Newspaper. The boats competed according to the following schedule. S-1 a 13 inch long sloop with fixed rudder. S2- a 15 inch long sloop with moveable rudder. M- a 24 linch long sloop with moveable rudder. And R- a 39 inch semi scale model of the America Cup Sloop with moveable rudder. The boats were raced on the Echo Park Lake. The boats were also judged for craftsmanship. I began by building the S class thirteen inch boat. It was made from a solid block of wood bandsawed to shape and then hollowed out with a gouge to a quarter inch wall thickness. The outside was then shaped and the deck, which was a single cedar shingle, was glued on. The mast was made from a strip of the shingle. The keel was cut from galvanized tin. A wooden plug was cut and formed for the keel weight and it was used to mold a weight from lead which was poured in a red sand mold with the tin inset. The hull was primered and painted with auto lacquer and the sails were made from broadcloth. I entered the boat and won my heat and first place in the final race. I received a trophy about 14 inches high and a case with a Speedway quarter inch drill and high speed grinder and attachments. My dad showed it to everybody that would look. My Mom was in the hospital for five continuous surgeries during this period so it was a great morale boost for him, he died a year later from complications from a peptic ulcer. My S2 boat was built the same way as the first, but I never entered it in competition because I was fully involved in an R class boat. I never built an M class boat although I wanted to but I just ran out of time in school. The R class boat was very complex. It was made from layers of 13/16 inch pine shelving. The layers were bandsawed to teardrop shape and glued together in a stack. The outside was shaped first and then the inside hollowed to quarter inch thickness. A chunk of wood bolted to the bottom was shaped to the keel weight size then removed and used as a mold plug in a red sand mold. Approximately five pounds of lead was used to pour the keel. It was then shaped to match the hull. The inside was coated with pitch and a mahoagany deck was glued on and shaped with crown and swoop. The metal work was added and the hull painted a Metallic Mexicalli Maroon. Mr. Hines was so proud of the boat he asked me to enter it in the Ford Industrial Awards. The model was crated up fully rigged because it was feared that no one would know how to rig it at the Ford Museum in Dearborn, Michigan. It won first place(I won a hundred dollars) it was then shipped to the Chicago Museum of Science and Industry where it was displayed for some time. I feared that it would not be home in time for the boat race at Echo Park, but luck brought it home and though damaged it was quickly repaired and Mr. Hines took us to Echo Park in his 37 Ford four door sedan to test them. We rowed a row boat all over chasing the models till we were all beat, but ready. On race day, Jamie Mitchell and I made it through the heats and in the finals we tangled on the start but then luck separated us and he won first and I won second. Later when the boats were judged I won first place craftsmanship and was presented a trophy by an unknown actor named Robert Mitchum. The second place trophy was wood and ten inches tall, the craftsmanship trophy was the same size and we were awarded ribbons and got out pictures in the newspaper. The boat was displayed at Luther Burbank Junior High and LA city schools District Offices. Because storage and transportation had caused damage to the hull they were sealed with fiberglass and refinished in 1991.

What it took to get there..........

ATP single and multi-engine
Commercial Rotorcraft Heli, single engine
Sea Private glider aero tow.
Certified flight instructor airplanes, instruments
Multi-engine. Ground and Advanced Instrument
Instructor.
Airframe and Powerplant Mechanic, Inspection
Authorization.
USAF Electronics Light Ground Communications
FCC General Class Radiotelephone
AA Electronics Glendale College CA
BS Aviation Maintenance Almeda College
MS Aviation Management Almeda College

Printed in the United States
By Bookmasters